THE HEART OF
THE CHRONICLES OF
NARNIA

KNOWING GOD HERE
BY FINDING HIM THERE

THOMAS WILLIAMS

W PUBLISHING GROUP
A Division of Thomas Nelson Publishers
Since 1798

www.wpublishinggroup.com

Published by W Publishing Group, a Division of Thomas Nelson, Inc., P.O. Box 141000, Nashville, Tennessee 37214.

W Publishing Group books may be purchased in bulk for educational, business, fundraising, or sales promotional use. For information, please e--mail SpecialMarkets@Thomas Nelson.com.

All Scripture quotations, unless otherwise indicated, are taken from the The New King James Version (NKJV®), copyright 1979, 1980, 1982, Thomas Nelson, Inc., Publishers. Used by permission. All rights reserved. Scripture quotations marked NLT are taken from the Holy Bible, New Living Translation, copyright © 1996. Used by permission of Tyndale House Publishers, Inc., Wheaton, Illinois 60189. All rights reserved.

Grateful acknowledgment to the C.S. Lewis Company for permission to quote from: THE MAGICIAN'S NEPHEW by C.S. Lewis, copyright © C.S. Lewis Pte. Ltd. 1955; THE LION, THE WITCH AND THE WARDROBE by C.S. Lewis, copyright © C.S. Lewis Pte. Ltd. 1950; THE HORSE AND HIS BOY by C.S. Lewis, copyright © C.S. Lewis Pte. Ltd. 1954; PRINCE CASPIAN by C.S. Lewis, copyright © C.S. Lewis Pte. Ltd. 1951; THE VOYAGE OF THE DAWN TREADER by C.S. Lewis, copyright © C.S. Lewis Pte. Ltd. 1952; THE SILVER CHAIR by C.S. Lewis, copyright © C.S. Lewis Pte. Ltd. 1953; THE LAST BATTLE by C.S. Lewis, copyright © C.S. Lewis Pte. Ltd. 1956; LETTERS TO CHILDREN by C.S. Lewis, copyright © C.S. Lewis Pte. Ltd. 1985; ON STORIES AND OTHER ESSAYS by C.S. Lewis, copyright © C.S. Lewis Pte. Ltd. 1966; MERE CHRISTIANITY by C.S. Lewis, copyright © C.S. Lewis Pte. Ltd. 1942, 1943, 1944, 1952; THE PROBLEM OF PAIN by C.S. Lewis, copyright © C.S. Lewis Pte. Ltd. 1940; THE WEIGHT OF GLORY by C.S. Lewis, copyright © C.S. Lewis Pte. Ltd. 1949.

Library of Congress Cataloging-in-Publication Data

Williams, T. M. (Thomas Myron), 1941-
    The Heart of the Chronicles of Narnia : knowing God here by finding him there / Thomas Williams.
        p. cm.
Includes bibliographical references.
    ISBN 0-8499-0488-9
    1. Lewis, C. S. (Clive Staples), 1898-1963. Chronicles of Narnia. 2. Children's stories, English—History and criticism. 3. Christian fiction, English—History and criticism. 4. Fantasy fiction, English—History and criticism. 5. Spiritual life in liter ature. 6. Narnia (Imaginary place) 7. God in literature. I. Title.
    PR6023.E926C5398 2005
    823'.912—dc22

                                                                    2005006154

Printed in the United States of America
05 06 07 08 09 RRD 9 8 7 6 5 4 3 2 1

To Larry and Reba Branum

CONTENTS

———

PART 1
THE STORY OF NARNIA

PART 2
LIVING LIKE A NARNIAN

PART 3
THE END AND THE BEGINNING

NOT A PUZZLE, BUT A FLOWER

C. S. Lewis's beloved *Chronicles of Narnia* are wonderfully imaginative tales that have thrilled and entertained readers of all ages for more than fifty years. Many who delight in this journey through Lewis's vivid imagination also sense deeper meanings lurking within the stories. And they are right; those meanings are there. Lewis's first intention, however, was not to teach lessons or burden readers with heavy insights, but simply to tell good stories. In a letter to an American girl he said, "I think that looking for a 'point' . . . may prevent one sometimes from getting the real effect of the story in itself."[1] He didn't want readers straining to read the stories as if they were puzzles to which they had to find solutions, but rather to approach each as "a flower whose smell reminds you of something you can't quite place."[2]

Yet the Narnia stories do have deeper meanings intricately woven into them. In a letter to a fifth-grade class in Maryland, Lewis revealed the seed from which all these meanings blossom when he said:

Let us suppose that there were a land like Narnia and that the Son of God, as He became a Man in our world, became a Lion there, and then imagine what would happen.[3]

Most readers who delight in the magic of Narnia also become eager to explore these underlying meanings, as well they should. Yes, Lewis believed readers should enjoy a story as a story before mining its insights, but that does not mean he thought those insights should not be mined. He himself was often the miner of such works as Milton's *Paradise Lost*, Spenser's *The Faerie Queene*, and dozens of others. His warning against looking for a point was simply to urge us to put first things first—to enjoy the stories first as stories and let the meanings emerge naturally as our minds open to them.

My purpose in this book is to help you flush out these insights and understand the deeper meanings after you have enjoyed *The Chronicles of Narnia* as pure pleasure. My method of exploration is first to let C. S. Lewis explain the stories himself, drawing on references from his other writings that illuminate the meaning of the Narnian passages and confirm his thought on given concepts. Second, I will confirm many Narnian principles with biblical references. Third, in a few instances I will draw on resources from other writers, but I believe that Lewis himself and Scripture provide most of the needed explanation.

Before you read this book, I hope you will first read the *Chronicles of Narnia* themselves. The last thing I want to do is destroy their marvelous beauty for you by turning them inside out and exposing Lewis's hand on the levers and pulleys. (Not to mention the fact that this book will give away much of the story plots and ruin the surprise of discovery.) If you have not read the *Chronicles*, lay this book aside right now, go read the stories, then come back and we'll explore their wonderful depth.

Before you enter Narnia, I will offer a bit of advice that you may find unnecessary. The seven books were originally numbered in the order in which they were written. When Lewis wrote *The Lion, the Witch and the Wardrobe*, he had no thought of writing the others. And when he did write them, it was not in the chronological order of Narnian history. Later editions of the series renumber the books in chronological order, but many older sets are still floating around, and people often ask me about their proper reading order. (Actually, the new numbering is somewhat controversial, with many readers preferring the original order.) In terms of enjoyment, it hardly matters. Each stands alone as its own complete story. But if you want to read them chronologically, here is the sequence: (1) *The Magician's Nephew*, (2) *The Lion, the Witch and the Wardrobe*, (3) *The Horse and His Boy*, (4) *Prince Caspian*, (5) *The Voyage of the Dawn Treader*, (6) *The Silver Chair*, (7) *The Last Battle*.

If you prefer to read them in the order they were written, here is the sequence: (1) *The Lion, the Witch, and the Wardrobe*, (2) *Prince Caspian*, (3) *The Voyage of the Dawn Treader*, (4) *The Silver Chair*, (5) *The Horse and His Boy*, (6) *The Magician's Nephew*, (7) *The Last Battle*.

When you return from Narnia, come back here, and we will delve into the meaning of the experience.

I gratefully acknowledge the influence of several people who helped bring *The Heart of the Chronicles of Narnia* into being and made it much better than my lone efforts would have. First I thank Laura Kendall and Greg Daniel of W Publishing Group for tapping me to write the book, as well as for their input in the initial shaping of it. I thank editor Evelyn Bence for her excellent work with me in pruning, correcting, and refining the final manuscript; proofreaders Sue Ann Jones and Bethany Bothman for their meticulous combing of the manuscript for grammatical and communication tangles; Gene Shelburne, Tommy Williams, and Chris Frizzell for their input on various theological issues; my wife, Faye, for the book's title, and designer Kirk DouPonce and illustrator Douglas Klauba for the excellent cover. All of you have my heartfelt gratitude.

—Thomas Williams

THE WORLD OF THE WARDROBE

The Narnian Phenomenon

> *I never wrote down to anyone; . . . it certainly is my opinion that a book worth reading only in childhood is not worth reading even then. The inhibitions which I hoped my stories would overcome in a child's mind may exist in a grown-up's mind too, and may perhaps be overcome by the same means.*
>
> —C. S. LEWIS, *ON STORIES AND OTHER ESSAYS ON LITERATURE*

As the twentieth century approached its midpoint, a bachelor in his fifties decided to write a story for children. One can hardly imagine a more unlikely writer. Clive Staples Lewis was a prominent Oxford academician, author of several scholarly books on English literature, a widely read Christian apologist noted for his formidable powers of reason and logic, and a man who had seldom been around children and admitted to being uncomfortable in their company. Yet from C. S. Lewis's pen flowed the *Chronicles of Narnia*, a series of seven children's stories that have earned a solid place on the shelf of enduring world classics alongside the works of Kenneth Grahame, A. A. Milne, Beatrix Potter, and Lewis Carroll. More than eighty-eight million Narnia books have been sold, and they have never been out of print.

The Narnia books are not merely read; they are absorbed. They affect many people deeply and become part of their psyches. Businesses, publishers, music groups, ministries, art studios, and wilderness treks bear the name of Narnia's main character, Aslan. Narnia has been the subject of many sermons, lectures, college courses, theater performances, master's theses, doctoral dissertations, and books. People name their Web sites, e-mail addresses, pets, and even their children for Narnian characters. I recently met a couple with a toddler named Rilian, after the prince in *The Silver Chair*. I have a grandson whose middle name is Caspian.

The phenomenal success of the *Chronicles of Narnia* is explained in part by the fact that its fans defy categorization. In my own family enthusiasm for the books spans four generations. My father was in his sixties when he first read them, and they became among his favorite Lewis writings. Thinking it unlikely that a stuffy Oxford don could write a compelling children's story, I did not venture into Narnia until I was in my thirties. But after the first book, I was hooked, and I soon read them all to my three grade-school daughters, who demanded a second reading not long afterward. I now have grandchildren who have devoured them.

The broad-based market for the Narnian stories confirms Lewis's premise that a good story is one that readers can enjoy at any age. He thought adult embarrassment at reading children's stories was silly; the essentials that make up a good story apply to all stories, whether written for an elementary-school girl or a sophisticated adult. "No book is really worth reading at the age of ten which is not equally (and often far more) worth reading at the age of fifty," he wrote.[1] He believed that growth and development in appreciation of literature should be like adding rings to a tree rather than like a train "leaving one station behind and puffing on to the next."[2]

Part of the error, as Lewis knew from his expertise in literature, was in thinking of fairy tales as a strictly children's genre. As J. R. R. Tolkien pointed out in his essay "On Fairy Tales," in most places and times fairy tales were not written for children but for adults. They presented in mythical form powerful truths worthy of consideration by the adult mind. G. K. Chesterton reminds us that stories such as "Beauty and the Beast" teach us "that a thing must be loved *before* it is lovable," a profound truth that says much about why God values us so highly. And he points out the power of the "'Sleeping Beauty' which tells how the human creature was blessed with all birthday gifts, yet cursed with death; and how death also may perhaps be softened into sleep."[3] Lewis tells us that the fairy tale "gravitated to the nursery when it became unfashionable in literary circles, just as unfashionable furniture gravitated to the nursery in Victorian houses."[4] Today publishers of imaginative tales for adults dealing with mythical or otherworldly creatures and magical events label such works fantasy or science fiction to avoid the juvenile association of the term *fairy tale.*

Many adults who still love, say, *The Wind in the Willows* might not be caught dead reading it on an airplane. But Lewis points out that such an attitude toward literature has nothing to do with whether the genre is worthy of adult reading. It reflects simply a desire to appear to have acquired adult tastes, which is in reality not a mature desire but a childish one.

> To be concerned about being grown up, to admire the grown up because it is grown up, to blush at the suspicion of being childish; these things are the marks of childhood and adolescence. . . . When I was ten, I read fairy tales in secret and would have been ashamed if I had been found doing so. Now that I am fifty I read them openly. When I became a man I put away childish things, including the fear of childishness and the desire to be very grown up.[5]

This acceptance and love of the fairy tale genre does much to explain Lewis's success in writing stories that appeal to such a wide range of ages. He never talked down to children. In fact he was astounded that any writer would do such a thing. He tells of a woman who sent him a manuscript of a children's story built around a mechanical gadget that, by pressing the right buttons, would give a child anything he or she wanted. Lewis had to tell the woman that he never cared much for this kind of story. She replied, "No more do I, it bores me to distraction. But it is what the modern child wants."[6] The woman was simply using good market strategy: find an audience and write a story to fit. Give the public what it wants no matter how little you like it yourself. Lewis could never write this way. When he wrote a children's story, he did not speak to his audience as a special category to be catered to but as a society of readers of which he was a part. The phenomenal success of Narnia shows that he knew what he was doing.

How Narnia Came to Be

How did this Oxford scholar come to write such highly successful children's stories? To answer we must go back to Lewis's childhood. Born in Belfast, Ireland, in 1898, Clive Staples Lewis disliked his name and early renamed himself Jack. He spent his boyhood in the company of his brother, Warren (Warnie), three years his senior, in a large house at the edge of the city. His parents were omnivorous readers who bought every book they read and never threw any away. The upper rooms were filled with books of every kind, which the boys devoured voraciously. Jack Lewis's favorite books were those of medieval knights or talking animals.

The brothers claimed an unfinished attic room as their domain and set up desks where they filled notebooks with stories set in their imaginary country of Boxen, a confederation combining Jack's Animal Land with Warnie's India. Many of Jack's stories were of animals, such as mice or rabbits in armor doing battle with evil cats. Others were political stories, featuring a frog named Lord Big, in a setting similar to nineteenth-century England.

When Lewis was nine, his mother died, destroying the happy

life of the Lewis family. Jack's grieving father abandoned the boys emotionally. He shipped them off to English boarding schools, causing long separations between the two brothers. Jack's extreme unhappiness in school, added to the emotional wrenching of his mother's death, turned him to atheism. His life regained some equilibrium under the tutelage of a brilliant scholar and logician, W. T. Kirkpatrick, who introduced the boy's eager mind to the rigors of logical thinking and successfully prepared him for entrance into Oxford University. Lewis became entrenched in his atheism (Kirkpatrick himself was a staunch unbeliever), but a ray of light penetrated his heart when he bought a cheap copy of George MacDonald's *Phantastes*, a nineteenth-century fantasy novel with strong but covert religious overtones. The book did not convert the young man; at the time he lacked the capacity to discern the source of its light. But he later wrote that reading MacDonald baptized his imagination. It revealed to him an undefined longing that lay deep in his heart.

After serving on the battle lines of France in World War I (where he was seriously wounded), Lewis took up his career as a university fellow at Oxford. There he established his famous lifelong friendship with Oxford don J. R. R. Tolkien. Volumes have been written about this close and productive friendship and the handful of men who clustered around them, forming the now legendary informal group, the Inklings. The group usually met twice each week, once in Lewis's college rooms and then at Oxford's Eagle and Child pub, to discuss philosophy and literature and read what they were currently writing for the group's opinion and critique.

The influence of Lewis and Tolkien on each other and the world of twentieth-century literature can hardly be overstated. Tolkien and fellow Inkling Hugo Dyson were largely responsible for converting Lewis to Christianity. Strange as it may seem, Tolkien used myth to bring Lewis to the truth. Reason had already led him to conclude intellectually that a god must exist, but he resisted Christianity's claim to be the one true religion. He could not see why it should not be considered just another among many nature religions with gods sacrificed and reborn to explain the cycle of the seasons. Tolkien appealed to Lewis's extensive knowledge of myth to convince him that the ancient myths were dim pictures in unenlightened minds groping for a central truth that was ultimately revealed in the historical fact of the incarnation and sacrifice of Christ. These myths were not really lies, but rough pictures prefiguring the truth that was revealed in the fact of Christianity—"myth became fact" as Lewis later explained it.

Tolkien's use of myth to convince Lewis of the truth is significant, because it shows the other powerful side of Lewis's mind: the imaginative side that thrived on story. Perhaps few minds in the twentieth century have held in such balance an incisive use of reason and logic alongside a rich imagination and devotion to story. These two highly developed attributes did much to make Lewis the most influential writer on Christianity in our time.

Lewis and Tolkien shared a deep love for imaginative story but found little worth reading in contemporary literature. Sometime in 1937, Lewis said to Tolkien, "Tollers, there is too little of what we really like in stories. I am afraid we shall have to write some ourselves."[7] From that challenge came Tolkien's *The Hobbit* and the three volumes of *The Lord of the Rings*, Lewis's science fiction trilogy *Out of the Silent Planet*, *Perelandra*, and *That Hideous Strength*, followed in the next decade by *Till We Have Faces* and the seven *Chronicles of Narnia*. The manuscripts-in-process of all these works were read aloud to meetings of the Inklings, who offered critiques and suggestions for improvement. Lewis wrote that, "Nobody influenced Tolkien. You may as well try to influence a bandersnatch."[8] Lewis biographer A. N. Wilson, however, claims that Lewis made an enormous contribution to bringing *The Lord of the Rings* into the world, going so far as to say that without Lewis it is unlikely that the trilogy would ever have been finished. Lewis acted as midwife to the epic, prodding and encouraging his procrastinating perfectionist friend to complete the work.[9]

Many Lewis readers assume that he must have contrived the

Narnian stories to make palatable certain lessons he wanted to teach. But neither Lewis nor Tolkien ever approached any work of fiction this way. They had strong and well-articulated convictions about what made good literature, one being that an author should never write a story with the idea of teaching a lesson. Yes, they believed that stories were ideal vehicles for illuminating great truths, but they insisted that the story came first, and any truth to be found would be that which germinated in the heart of the author and percolated naturally into the story.[10] Any other approach would show itself to be false as a story and unable to camouflage its true colors—a sermon in disguise.

As Lewis explained in many of his letters and in a short essay, "The *Lion* all began with a picture of a Faun carrying an umbrella and parcels in a snowing wood. This picture had been in my mind since I was about sixteen. Then one day when I was about forty, I said to myself: 'Let's try to make a story about it.'" Lewis had little idea as to how the story would go until "suddenly Aslan came bounding into it."[11] In another essay he explained that the various images that came to him began to form and sort themselves into a story. At this point there was nothing specifically Christian about the story, but as ideas bubbled in his mind, "that element pushed itself in of its own accord."[12] As he mulled over the shape and developing content of the story, he decided that the fairy tale was the ideal form in which these elements could be expressed.

Although he had begun *The Lion, the Witch and the Wardrobe* in 1939, he abandoned it until late 1948 and finished it sometime before the spring of 1949. It was published in 1950. At first he had no thought of a sequel, much less a series, though the idea of other books must have come to him before he completed *Lion*, for in the last paragraph we have a sure hint that a sequel is coming. Lewis dashed off the next six books in rapid-fire order, and in March 1953 he told his publisher, Geoffrey Bles, that he had completed the seventh and last book, *The Last Battle*. Bles wisely chose to release the books at the rate of one per year, and thus all were in stores by 1956.

THE TRUTH ABOUT FAIRY TALES

Although millions of Christians have delighted in the Narnia stories, I have encountered several and heard of others who shy away from any form of fantasy literature containing magic or real-world impossibilities. They mistrust such stories as conveyors of truth or fear them as escapism from reality. Lewis himself encountered the same attitude and effectively laid to rest such objections by showing how such tales can be "truer" than much of what children read in contemporary fiction. He believed that adults tend not to give children enough credit for discerning the difference between the actual and the fantastic—that no child is deceived into thinking fairy tales are real. He felt that what professed to be realistic stories for children were more apt to deceive or tempt them into the worst kind of escapism, leading them to imagine themselves to be the football hero, the class beauty, the winner of every school contest and honor—goals not technically impossible but infinitely improbable for all but a select few. "I never expected the real world to be like the fairy tales," he wrote. "I think that I did expect school to be like the school stories. The fantasies did not deceive me: the school stories did."[13] He saw the way in which the realistic story addresses wish fulfillment as dangerous and egocentric. Children run to them to escape the humiliation and disappointments they encounter in the real world. The pleasure they get consists of picturing themselves as the objects of admiration—all flattery to the ego.

The longing aroused by the fantastic tale is quite different. The boy reading such a story does not really desire the dangers of dragons and giants and ogres and enchanters. His desire is diffused over the entire world he enters, and it's impossible to identify any single object as the focus of it. The whole magical aura of castles, knights, spells, woods, mist-shrouded mountains, dwarfs, caves, courage, and honor draws him. As Lewis said, "It stirs him and troubles him (to his life-long enrichment) with the dim sense of something beyond his reach and, far from dulling or emptying the actual world, gives it a new dimension of depth. He does not despise real woods because he has read of enchanted woods: the reading makes all real woods a little enchanted."[14]

Addressing the charge that fantasy literature is escapism, Tolkien asked Lewis, "What class of men would you expect to be most preoccupied with, and most hostile to, the idea of escape?" The answer: *jailers.*[15] Lewis described the Christian life as warfare in which Christians lived in enemy-occupied territory. Naturally our enemies would oppose our escape; they would condemn any sort of reading that opens the door and shows us the glory of our true commander, inspiring us to rally to him and throw off the yoke of oppression.

PAST THE WATCHFUL DRAGONS

As the ideas for *The Lion, the Witch and the Wardrobe* bubbled in Lewis's mind, he began to see how such a story could reveal the truth about Christianity in the same way that fairy tales reveal the magical wonder of the natural world. A story could bypass inhibitions that common attitudes toward religion impose on the mind. He noted that

> reverence itself did harm. The whole subject [religion] was associated with lowered voices; almost as if it were something medical. But supposing that by casting all these things into an imaginary world, stripping them of their stained-glass and Sunday school associations, one could make them for the first time appear in their real potency? Could one not thus steal past those watchful dragons? I thought one could.[16]

Here is where Narnia shines and reveals its greatness. Great art, whether story, painting, music, or drama, distills the essence of reality. It makes us see the truth and feel the emotion that we bury under the routine, schedules, deadlines, humdrum, hurry, and clamor of our everyday lives. Lewis believed that one of the functions of art is "to present what the narrow and desperately practical perspectives of real life exclude."[17] Just as a magnifying glass concentrates sunrays, so art concentrates the diverse beams on which our lives run to reveal the grandeur of truth underlying the mundane—the beauty and magnificence that has been lurking in reality all along, invisible to us because of our distractions. And the gift keeps on giving, for once the hidden beauty and truth are revealed, they linger. We bring them from the book, the painting, or the symphony into the real world where they bathe the ordinary with magic and make common things glow with ethereal light.

Our problem is that, in Harry Potter terms, we have become "muggles"—mundane creatures unappreciative of and denying the power of anything we cannot see, hear, feel, taste, or touch. Modern rationalism and everyday routine have worn us down to where we reject the magical, romantic view of reality as head-in-the-clouds fantasy. We smile indulgently at teen crushes that send young people swooning and dreaming of that one face that entrances all the senses. We warn about-to-be-marrieds not to expect the euphoria of palpitating romance to last. Romance is an illusion caused by stars in the eyes. We tell the couple to expect the romance to fade and warn them to steel themselves for the long-haul, everyday chore of making a marriage work. *Work* is the key, not romance. Not joy.

Of course these are all sensible warnings because we live in a fallen world. We are flawed. The new wears off. Youthful beauty fades. The travails we experience convince us that wonder and romance are illusions, that plodding duty and hard work express the essence of reality.

Not so. In the play as God originally wrote it, the euphoria and tingling romance were intended to last. Wonder and delight are essential ingredients of reality, deeply embedded beneath the canker and rust that have marred the world since creation. Beneath the crust of decay, immense glory resides latent in every created thing. That beauty is still visible to any eyes that can be opened to see it. Chesterton reminded us that our world is just as much a fantastic creation as any that the most imaginative fantasy writer can devise. The romantic view is the true view of reality, because it sees beyond the veil to the true heart of a thing. When the face we behold across the candlelit table appears to be that of a goddess, we see the truth. Likewise when the mountain looks like a monumental being aspiring toward heaven, when the chord of music reverberates in the heart and fills us with a longing for we know not what. In these magical moments the truth breaks past our defenses, shows our muggle existence to be a lie, and reveals reality in all its glory for what it really is.

I think this is the real explanation for Narnia's phenomenal worldwide popularity. The essence of Christianity and what the Incarnation was about have been largely obscured beneath a layer of hushed holiness, legalism, perfunctory ritual, and propositional dogma. As a result, religion has so little general appeal that many reject it altogether. But when we go to Narnia, we don't see "religion" at all. Instead we see a country full of joy, love, beauty, grandeur, homey simplicity, and goodwill that is created and ruled by a magnificent and desirable creature who is powerful, gentle, loving, stern, playful, just, sacrificial, forgiving, and protective. Within and without, the land faces deadly enemies who can be defeated by the courage of its inhabitants and the providence of its great leader. None of these qualities are presented as religion, but they show us the essence of what religion ought to be in our world. It is not church attendance, study, law, ritual, teaching, or belief. These things are the dressing, the shell, the outer wall. The essence of religion is not a category of life; it is the truth about reality itself. It is living a life of joy and courage in community under a loving leader who has our good at heart.

This kind of life shows clearly and in all its glory in Narnia. When we close the last book, we see our own world with new eyes — eyes with the muggle scales sloughed off to reveal the truth of reality in all its romantic glory.

We still have our rituals, but now they take on deep meaning. We see them, not as the essence of religion, but as pointers toward the essence. Law is still important, but it is a loving guide to joy rather than a restrictive demand. Church is no longer a burdensome meeting but a loving community of mutual support and rapport with people bonded by a common purpose. Jesus is no longer a distant, historical, insipid, meek and mild, otherworldly figure who offers salvation but has nothing to do with my everyday world; he becomes a living, magnificent, robust, manly being who offers infinite joy and the deepest love a human can ever know. We see the truth more clearly because Narnia strips away the incrustation and shows us its essence.

———•◦•———

PART 1

THE STORY OF NARNIA

CHAPTER 1

NOT A TAME LION
The Truth about God

It's not as if he were a tame lion.
—CORIAKIN THE ISLAND MAGICIAN,
THE VOYAGE OF THE DAWN TREADER

———————

It is the darkest days of World War II, and London is under heavy attack. The British government urges parents to send their children out of the city for safety. Peter, Susan, Edmund, and Lucy Pevensie, brothers and sisters, have been sent to the country estate of old Professor Kirke. To their great delight, the professor leaves the children to themselves and gives them free run of most of his huge manor.

Soon after settling in, the four siblings explore the house. They wander through spare bedrooms, stairways, balconies, and galleries hung with rich curtains and filled with books, old paintings, suits of armor, and even a harp. Little do they know that things are about to change from the ordinary to the extraordinary.

One room is empty except for a dead bluebottle fly on the window sill and a large wardrobe. Three of the children traipse on through the room. But Lucy, the youngest, is curious about the wardrobe and lingers behind to check it out. Loving the feel of the fur coats she finds when she opens the door, she steps inside. Going deeper, she finds a second row of coats and, after that, something crunchy beneath her feet and the scraping of twigs against her face.

She has gone through the wardrobe into a snow-covered wood. Now even more curious, Lucy walks toward a lone lamppost she sees in the distance and, to her great surprise, encounters a creature half goat and half man—Tumnus the faun. He tells her that she is in Narnia, an archaic kingdom under the spell of the evil White Witch who has inflicted permanent winter upon it.

Not long afterward Lucy's brothers and sister follow her through the wardrobe, and the four children begin their adventures in Narnia. Soon a talking beaver intercepts them and warns them of grave danger. He draws them close and whispers: "They say Aslan is on the move—perhaps has already landed." The children have no idea who Aslan is, but the very name gives them strange sensations.

> Peter felt suddenly brave and adventurous. Susan felt as if some delicious smell or some delightful strain of music had just floated by her. And Lucy got the feeling you have when you wake up in the morning and realize that it is the beginning of the holidays or the beginning of summer.[1]

When all are safe and snug in the beaver's cozy hut, the children ask about Aslan.

"Aslan?" Mr. Beaver replies. "Why don't you know? He's the King. He's the Lord of the whole wood, but not often here, you understand." The Beaver goes on to explain: "Aslan is a lion—*the* Lion, the great Lion." Mrs. Beaver adds,

> "If there's anyone who can appear before Aslan without their knees knocking, they're either braver than most or else just silly."
> "Then he isn't safe?" said Lucy.
> "Safe?" said Mr. Beaver. ". . . Who said anything about safe? 'Course he isn't safe. But he's good. He's the King, I tell you."[2]

Mr. Beaver has been charged with leading Peter and his two

sisters to meet Aslan. And when they meet him, they are not prepared for what they see.

> People who have not been in Narnia sometimes think that a thing cannot be good and terrible at the same time. If the children had ever thought so, they were cured of it now. For when they tried to look at Aslan's face they just caught a glimpse of the golden mane and the great, royal, solemn, overwhelming eyes; and then they found they couldn't look at him and went all trembly.[3]

The children are hesitant to approach the magnificent but fearsome creature, and each tries to shove the other forward. Finally Peter, being the oldest, realizes it is up to him. He musters up his courage, steps toward the Lion, and says, "We have come—Aslan."

Thus in the pages of C. S. Lewis's *The Lion, the Witch and the Wardrobe*, human children find God in Narnia in the form of a lion, as children and adults have been doing for more than fifty years. The great Lion Aslan has characteristics much like our own Christ, and of course the resemblance is not accidental. For two generations this Christlike being in a form and setting so different from the real Christ has softened the resistance of many to religion and shown the essence of God with an unexpected freshness that breaks through mental barriers.

Of all the ways to depict a type of Christ, why did Lewis choose a lion? When you think about it, in a world of talking animals, what could be more natural than for the Christ figure to be an animal? And if an animal, what is more natural than a lion—the king of beasts, a symbol for strength, and surely the most noble looking of all beasts? If you are like me, when you think of God the Father, you picture him as a superhuman man. Animals, if they had rationality, would surely imagine their god as a super edition of an animal like themselves. As Dorothy Sayers said, "If a clam could conceive of God, it would conceive of Him in the shape of a great, big clam."[4]

Does it dishonor God to portray him as an animal? Perhaps we should first ask if it dishonors God to think of him as a man. Some high-minded people have trouble with the idea that God could take on the form of any of his creatures, including humans. The warhorse Bree in *The Horse and His Boy* speaks for these people when the young princess Aravis asks him if Aslan is really a lion.

> "No, no, of course not," said Bree in a rather shocked voice. . . .
>
> "No doubt," continued Bree, "when they speak of him as a Lion they only mean that he's as strong as a lion or . . . as fierce as a lion. . . . It would be quite absurd to suppose he is a real lion. Indeed it would be disrespectful. If he was a lion he'd have to be a Beast just like the rest of us. Why!" (and here Bree began to laugh) "If he was a lion he'd have four paws, and a tail, and *Whiskers!*"[5]

But of course Bree is wrong. In the next moment he finds himself face to face with Aslan and discovers that he *does* have four paws, a tail, and whiskers. The Lion Aslan affirms Narnia's God as a flesh-and-blood reality, reflecting Lewis's certainty of the incarnation of God as a real man in our world. In *Mere Christianity* he wrote, "The Second Person in God, the Son, became human Himself: was born into the world as an actual man—a real man of a particular height, with hair of a particular colour, speaking a particular language, weighing so many stone."[6]

One of the perks of having a God like ourselves is that we can identify with him emotionally. He is one of us and has a body like other people with whom we love and laugh and cry. Incarnation puts a face on God and allows him to become real to us. In the Narnian land of rational animals, a lion serves the same purpose.

If additional justification is needed for portraying God as a lion, we need look no further than the Bible itself. In the apostle John's great vision on Patmos, one of the twenty-four elders sitting around God's throne explains that the "Lion of the tribe of Judah" has opened the great scroll in the hand of God.[7] Throughout the Bible the lion is often a symbol of strength and nobility. The apostle thought it appropriate to use such a creature as an image of God.

NOT A MAP, BUT A PORTRAIT

No doubt you have read books or attended Sunday school classes about God where you got an analytical approach that dissected him and labeled his various known attributes—his omnipotence, omniscience, omnipresence, infiniteness, eternal existence, and trinitarian nature. This kind of study we call *theology*, and it gives us valuable help in comprehending a being far beyond our capacity to understand. In *Mere Christianity* Lewis compares theology to a map of the ocean. Studying a map is not nearly as much fun as sailing the sea, but the map is necessary if you want to get to another continent.[8]

Many become so involved with the map, however, that they neglect the ocean. It is possible to study diligently all the characteristics of God until one knows much *about* him without ever coming to know *him*.

That is the first place where the *Chronicles of Narnia* help us. Instead of plotting another map of God, these stories paint a picture of him. Instead of analysis we get a portrait. It's much like the dictum every journalism teacher drums into her students: "Show, don't tell." Don't waste words telling your readers how they ought to feel; *make them feel it*. When the great Lion Aslan comes bounding into Narnia, we don't get a breakdown of God's components; we experience a vivid presence glowing with personality, power, tenderness, compassion, and grandeur. In Aslan we are not told about the nature of God; we are shown it so vividly that we almost feel we are experiencing him firsthand.

What Aslan Shows Us about God

No doubt you have heard people say, "I can't believe in a God who would condemn anyone to hell or allow an infant child to be taken from its mother. I believe in a God of love who wants people to be happy." We tend to look for a safe, tame, benevolent God who is kind to us, and we have convinced ourselves that God wants us to feel safe, secure, and immersed in the affluent life that we have come to expect as the norm in America. Many people have no qualms about using their prayers to bend him to their will. Often those prayers are little more than want lists presented to him as if he were a shopping mall Santa. These people have tamed their God into a nice, safe, and kind figure who accepts us where we are, and though he wishes we would do better, he sighs, smiles indulgently, and does not demand it.

But in Aslan we encounter an altogether different kind of God. "It's not as if he were a tame lion," the island magician tells Lucy.[9] He is not the pushover God of modern evangelicalism. No one can control him. We can't bend him to our wills and remake him into what we want him to be. In Aslan Lewis undermines the notion that God wants us safe, happy, and content on our own terms.

In *The Silver Chair* the schoolgirl Jill finds herself alone and terribly thirsty in an unknown woods. She comes upon a stream, but between her and the water sits the great Lion. Though her thirst is overpowering, she stops in her tracks, too fearful to advance or to run.

"If you're thirsty, you may drink," says the Lion.

The terrified Jill wants assurance that she will not be eaten. "Will you promise not to—do anything to me, if I do come?" she asks.

"I make no promise," the Lion answers.

"I daren't come and drink," Jill replies.

"Then you will die of thirst," the Lion tells her. When Jill says she will go and look for another stream, the Lion responds, "There is no other stream."[10]

In the end Jill musters up the courage to step forward and

drink, though it is the hardest thing she has ever done. The God of Narnia cannot be manipulated by human wants. The Lion knows that Jill needs water, and he wants her to have it. But she wants it on her own terms, which means avoiding him and getting a guarantee of safety. Aslan knows that Jill's terms for happiness will not achieve her ultimate good. She wants fulfillment without encountering God, and fulfillment on those terms is impossible. Aslan ignores her desire for comfort and safety, insisting that she take the necessary risk of encountering God as the ultimate satisfaction of all needs and desires.

God wants you to be fulfilled and happy—indeed he wants you to be ecstatically and deliriously happy—happier than you can possibly be on your own terms. All complaints against his severity boil down to this: "If God really wants me to be happy, he will give me exactly what I want." But as Lewis explains elsewhere, "It is just no good asking God to make us happy in our own way without bothering about religion. God cannot give us a happiness and peace apart from Himself, because it is not there."[11] We are created to find happiness only in him, and he does all he can to turn us away from our fearful and self-seeking selves toward him so we can find the joy for which he created us. This is the truth about God that Peter and his sisters discover when they first face Aslan. Though they are at first afraid to approach him because he is clearly both good and terrible, they find the courage to do it. And after the Lion's welcome, they no longer feel awkward but glad and quiet. When they face his severity, they find his love.

LOVE AND SEVERITY

Aslan of Narnia at first seems a more severe deity than our Christ because he never lets his people off the hook. He allows pain, places hard tasks on his subjects, and accepts no excuses for their failures. When Aslan asks the three children why their brother is not with them, the Beaver explains that Edmund has betrayed them. Peter feels compelled to say, "That was partly my fault, Aslan. I was angry with him and I think that helped him to go wrong."[12] Aslan does not excuse Peter but merely looks at him with his great golden eyes. The Lion shows similar severity in the other stories. In *The Horse and His Boy* Aslan inflicts scratches on the back of the girl Aravis to punish her for mistreatment of a servant. In *Prince Caspian* Lucy is astounded that Aslan expects her to follow him into the darkness of an uncharted wilderness even if it means leaving her brothers and sister who refuse to follow. The Lion demands to be obeyed at all costs. Extenuating circumstances, extreme difficulty, or emotional trauma are not excuses.

Narnia readers who find this portrait of God bothersome may have forgotten the severity of Christ's call. "If you want to be my follower you must love me more than your own father and mother, wife and children, brothers and sisters—yes, more than your own life. . . . And you cannot be my disciple if you do not carry your own cross and follow me."[13] The kind and indulgent God so often presented to us today is not authentic. As Lewis points out in *The Problem of Pain*, these days when people speak of God's goodness, they really mean his love, which they interpret as kindness. "What would really satisfy us would be a God who said of anything we happened to like doing, 'What does it matter so long as they are contented?'" But, as Lewis goes on to explain, God is not like that: "Love is something more stern and splendid than mere kindness. . . . Kindness, merely as such, cares not whether its object becomes good or bad, provided only that it escapes suffering."[14]

If to spare us pain and discomfort God allows evil to continue in us, he is not loving. Kindness gives in and cuts us some slack while love holds our feet to the fire until it accomplishes what is best for our ultimate well-being. Kindness removes obstacles to our contentment while love remakes us into what we are intended to be. This remaking is far from comfortable. It often requires tearing out walls and scraping away mold and rot before rebuilding. But this is what God does. He loves us so much that he will cut out the cancer or pull the tooth in spite of our pain. He wants so much for us to share eternal life with him that he is determined to burn out of our souls everything that is not eternal, even if we are painfully scorched in the process.

THE OTHER SIDE OF SEVERITY

Instead of kindness Aslan sometimes offers severity, but in every instance his severity is ultimately revealed as love. And the many scenes in all the stories showing the warmth and tenderness of Aslan give us a picture of God's love so magnetic and appealing that we can understand why many children fall in love with Jesus after meeting the Lion. After explaining to Aravis why he clawed her back, Aslan gently invites her to draw near to him and experience the love of his now-velveted paws. When Digory in *The Magician's Nephew* works up the nerve to ask Aslan to give him something to cure his mother, to his great wonder he sees tears in the Lion's eyes. "They were such big, bright tears compared with Digory's own that for a moment he felt as if the Lion must really be sorrier about his Mother than he was himself."[15] When Lucy meets Aslan after failing to follow him alone, he greets her with warmth and love. "The great beast rolled over on his side so that Lucy fell, half sitting and half lying between his front paws. He bent forward and just touched her nose with his tongue. His warm breath came all round her."[16]

In many instances Jesus showed the same kind of tender love and compassion. As he approached the tomb of Lazarus, Jesus knew that in a matter of moments he would call the man back to life. Yet the sight of the grieving sisters so touched his heart that he broke down and cried.[17] Aslan's gentle affection to Lucy demonstrates what Jesus longed to do with the resistant Jewish people when he cried, "O Jerusalem, Jerusalem, the one who kills the prophets and stones those who are sent to her! How often I wanted to gather your children together, as a hen gathers her chicks under her wings, but you were not willing!"[18] At the Last Supper Jesus spoke with great tenderness to his disciples, those stubborn, dense, bickering, and faltering men (just like you and me) he chose as his closest companions. "As the Father loved Me, I also have loved you. . . . No longer do I call you servants, for a servant does not know what his master is doing; but I have called you friends."[19]

Does such language astound you as it does me? We ordinary, bumbling, sin-prone humans can be *friends*, of all things, with the Creator and Ruler of the universe. He cherishes us. He delights in us. He wants to be with us and longs to have us love him in return. In Narnia Aslan shows this love of God up close and personal in such a way that we cannot possibly miss the truth.

In the original scheme of things, God willed that humans enjoy a life filled with nothing but goodness, love, and joy. He intended us to be happy and never wanted evil or pain to afflict us. But when evil entered not only the world but our own hearts as well, he determined to perform the painful surgery necessary to remove from our lives the root cause of all pain. Narnia makes the purpose of this painful operation clear to us. The stories show us why Aslan must allow pain and ask for sacrificial acts and choices. But they also show us the other side of God in the many scenes of warm and tender love of Aslan for his creatures. It is a beautiful picture of Jesus and his love for us.

In Narnia the good creatures respond to Aslan's love by loving him in return. A fine example occurs near the end of *The Lion, the Witch and the Wardrobe* when Aslan and his army invade the castle of the White Witch to free the Narnians she has captured and turned to stone. Aslan breathes on each of the figures, and life returns to them. Among them is another lion, who, after being restored to life, cannot resist the great Lion and goes bounding after him, frisking around him with delight and licking his face. The released lion cannot contain his desire to be near Aslan and express his love.

It's a little harder for us to feel or express our love for Jesus, because we no longer have him among us in physical form, and we can't hear him talking to us in a real human voice. It's easier to love those around us whom we can see, touch, and hear. But a time is coming when we will be freed from our imprisonment in this fallen world, and we will be able to see face to face the Jesus who freed us. At that time you will feel exactly as this released lion did. You will be unable to contain your joy as you look on his dear face. At that moment you will see in Jesus everything you now see in your dearest beloved, but intensified beyond your wildest imagining. When you see him, you will know that he is and has been the One you have always loved more than anything else in your life.

The trick is to experience the exhilaration of that kind of love now. The *Chronicles of Narnia* make it a little easier by showing that kind of love modeled in Aslan and the creatures who love him.

CHAPTER 2

THE SONG OF ASLAN
The Creation of Narnia

I give you forever this land of Narnia. I give you the woods, the
fruits, the rivers. I give you the stars and I give you myself.
—ASLAN, THE MAGICIAN'S NEPHEW

———◦·••·◦———

A strange assortment of five people and one horse are suddenly pulled out of a melee in Victorian London and plunged into utter darkness. Two children, Digory and Polly, have used a set of magical rings to accomplish this feat, hoping to stop the riot by removing an evil witch from another dimension whom they have brought into the city. But in the process they inadvertently take more people out of the world than they intend. Now the group, consisting of the two children, Digory's uncle, the witch, a cabby, and his horse, stand bewildered in a dark and empty world. After several moments of confusion, the group stops short. A faraway voice is singing. Though the song has no words, it is the most beautiful sound Digory has ever heard. "Sometimes it seemed to come from all directions at once. Sometimes he almost thought it was coming out of the earth beneath them. Its lower notes were deep enough to be the voice of the earth herself."[1]

As the song continues, an uncountable chorus of silver voices joins in, and the blackness overhead blazes with stars, constellations, and planets. The chorus drops away, and the single voice swells to a mighty sound as a light begins to glow before the watching group, revealing a bare horizon. The light increases until a huge sun appears. The watchers gape in awe as the sun reveals the singer—a great, golden lion. The Lion begins to pace, and his song becomes softer and more lilting. Grass spreads across the ground, covering the bare earth like a wave. Trees sprout from the earth and grow to full height in minutes. The song continues, and animals, birds, and insects of all shapes and sizes emerge from the ground, braying, barking, and trumpeting all about the astonished group.

THE VOICE OF GOD

Compare this account of the creation of Narnia with the creation of our world in Genesis. There we read that God spoke and things came into existence—light, vegetation, stars, planets, and all the earth's creatures. God speaks, whereas Aslan sings, but in each case it's the voice of Deity that brings about creation. Of course none of us really knows what it means that God spoke and creation occurred. The Genesis account may be a simplification of what really happened, giving us only the end result of it. Nevertheless, in the creation of Narnia we feel as if we are getting an up-close picture of what might have occurred when the voice of God called creation into existence.

The song of Aslan also resonates with other instances in the Bible where inanimate creation responds to God's voice. Jesus commands the winds to be still, and a storm ceases. He forbids a fig tree ever to grow fruit again, and it withers. If you think it's fanciful that the stars sing with Aslan in Narnia, remember God asking Job where he was "When the morning stars sang together, / And all the sons of God shouted for joy?"[2] As Jesus enters Jerusalem, the Pharisees urge him to silence the earsplitting welcome of the joyful crowd. He answers, "I tell you that if these should keep silent, the stones would immediately cry out."[3]

Stars singing and stones shouting are metaphoric exaggerations for emphasis, no doubt—or are they? Is it possible that inanimate things can praise God? Have you looked up into the nighttime sky on a clear night and found the stars so vivid that they seemed to make *all* your senses come alive? You did not really hear any sound coming from the heavens, yet somehow you sensed the presence of a tingling harmony, seemingly on the edge of hearing, that filled the silence above like something alive. I don't claim that stars can literally sing or that stones can yell, yet something in these images strikes a chord in us, and we find ourselves wondering if more than metaphor could be at work here. Don't you sometimes sense some inexpressible meaning just beneath the surface of all things that seems to be speaking to you?

Before you answer no, think again of a young man gazing across the restaurant table at his fiancée's face glowing magically in the soft candlelight. I trust you have experienced the same thing yourself (if not, I hope you will). Your heart beats faster, your breath comes deeper, and you are enthralled by this heavenly vision of the most beautiful creature you have ever seen. And within that face you see a soul just as beautiful and dream of all the joys and delights of spending a lifetime with her. If you dismiss these exhilarating feelings as a temporary, infatuated, romantic illusion with no basis in reality, as the muggles encourage you to do, you will miss out on a great truth that can bathe the rest of your life in glory. It is in those magical, romantic moments that you see reality as God created reality to be and intended it to remain. The fading of beauty with age, the dimming of the romantic glow, the pain and hard work that go with keeping the marriage alive when the blossom withers are not the truth about creation. They comprise the blight that has marred reality as God created it. If sin had not corrupted all things, the beauty, romance, and euphoria of lovers would last forever. And we would see the same entrancing glory not only in our lover's eyes but also in all creation. That is the reality that shouts to you through all created things.

THE SPEAKER AND THE WORD

More than once the Narnian stories identify Aslan as the Son of the Emperor-beyond-the-Sea. He is parallel to Jesus rather than to God the Father. Here Lewis reflects Scripture in making Aslan the key figure in the creation story. The apostle John tells us that the Son was in the beginning with God, and that "all things were made through Him, and without Him nothing was made that was made."[4]

I find it significant to the creation story that the gospel of John identifies Jesus as "the Word." Just as words are emanations from a speaker that give form to his thought and display his mind, the Son is the emanation from God that gives form to his thought and displays his nature. He is God expressed in tangible form. He is the Word that God speaks, the One who brings ideas from the creative mind of God into tangible existence. As Aslan sings, he is the voice bringing the Narnian world into existence, the tangible expression of God's mind, the creative Word of God in action. The mind of the Emperor-beyond-the-Sea is revealed audibly and visibly in Aslan, and through his word worlds come into existence.

THE RATIONAL CREATURES

After completing the creation of Narnia, Aslan calls out certain pairs of beasts from the rest and speaks to them saying, "Awake. Love. Think. Speak. Be walking trees. Be talking beasts. Be divine waters."[5] Immediately the creatures respond. Fauns, satyrs, dwarfs, dryads of the trees, naiads of the river, and all the beasts and birds that Aslan called out speak with articulate voices. He has given them reason, speech, and free will.

Along with the gift of speech and rationality comes a responsibility.

"Creatures, I give you yourselves," said the strong, happy voice of Aslan. "I give to you forever this land of Narnia. I give you

the woods, the fruits, the rivers. I give you the stars and I give
you myself. The Dumb Beasts whom I have not chosen are
yours also. Treat them gently and cherish them but do not go
back to their ways lest you cease to be Talking Beasts."[6]

No human is created in Narnia, but humans are quickly "im-
ported" from our earth. One member of the party pulled into Narnia
is a wise and honest young London cabby; Aslan calls the man's wife
into his new world and crowns them as King Frank and Queen
Helen. He tells them that they will be father and mother of many
kings that will rule Narnia and Archenland for generations to come.

Aslan's charge to Frank and Helen and the talking beasts
reminds us of God's charge to the first couple on earth. After creat-
ing Adam and Eve, "God blessed them, and God said to them,
'Be fruitful and multiply; fill the earth and subdue it; have dominion
over the fish of the sea, over the birds of the air, and over every
living thing that moves on the earth.'"[7] Humans are placed in charge
of Narnia just as humans were placed in charge of earth. As
Trufflehunter, the badger in *Prince Caspian*, says, "Narnia was never
right except when a son of Adam was King."[8]

CARETAKERS OF THE EARTH

God's charge to Adam and Eve to care for the earth and respect
nature is still our charge as their descendants. It is part of our function as humans—one of the tasks for which we were created. And in
Narnia we find what it means for humans to care for the world and
have dominion over the animals. Narnia is a land in harmony with
nature. Humans and the rational creatures rule the natural resources
and the dumb animals with a benevolent headship that balances
utility with protection. The use of resources is always based on need
rather than greed.

In every Narnia book we see nature used but not abused. Dwarfs mine the earth and create beautiful artifacts, but they produce only what they can make with their hands. There are no mass-production assembly lines consuming irreplaceable resources to belch out little-needed products to enhance appearance, increase luxury, or improve status. Cows and goats are milked, horses are ridden, reindeer pull sleighs, stones and timbers are cut to build cottages and castles, and dumb beasts are hunted for food. But all are cared for and valued. Nature is a cherished servant, not an abused slave. In Narnia all the good, rational creatures obviously love their world and respect it. And the key to our fulfilling our charge as rulers over nature is to see it with the same loving eyes as these Narnians.

Beauty and Goodness

No doubt one reason that Aslan chooses the cabby Frank as the first king of Narnia is the young man's sensitivity to goodness and beauty. He is a true romantic. As the Lion sings his creation song, two other members of the party, Digory's uncle Andrew and the witch, cause a commotion, trying to take from Digory the magic rings that would return them to earth. Frank has every reason to be just as confused and fearful as they are. He, too, has suddenly been thrust into an unformed world he didn't even know existed. Yet he forgets his plight because he is spellbound by the magnificent Lion and his song. He tells the squabblers to hold their noise; he wants to hear the music. When the stars appear and burst into song, he exclaims, "Glory be!" and says, "I'd ha' been a better man all my life if I'd known there were things like this."[9]

Of course there were "things like this" back in Frank's world. His English sky was as filled with wonders as the Narnian sky, but in the hustle and humdrum of London life, his latent sensitivity to beauty was smothered beneath the everyday necessity of eking out a living with his horse and cab. Narnia, however, does the same thing for him that it does for us. It eliminates the distractions and reawakens the wonder, leading us to sense that music of the spheres that we can't quite hear.

Notice that as Frank watches creation in progress, he feels the desire to be a better man. He connects all he witnesses with the idea of goodness. He wants to be good because he longs to be part of what is going on about him, and he rightly senses that all of it is supremely good. The Narnian stories affirm that the material creation is good. They stand in stark contrast to ancient heresies that claim spirit to be good and matter evil. In the Genesis creation story, God himself at the end of each day pronounced his day's work to be good. And at the end of the sixth day, he surveyed the entire panorama, including the beautiful naked bodies of the man and woman, "and indeed it was very good."[10]

Although Genesis and classical Christian thought affirm the goodness of the material creation, shades of those ancient heresies still linger in the minds of many—the idea of a sharp division between the physical and the spiritual, with the spiritual by far the superior and the physical of little worth or even leaning toward the bad. Many see the earth as having no permanent value because it is merely a physical place and our ultimate destination is heaven, an idyll of pure spirituality. They think the body has no ultimate importance because it will wear down and die, leaving us as spirits inhabiting some kind of vaguely conceived, nonphysical body in heaven.

Narnia stands in stark contrast to this negative view of physical matter. Many of Lewis's other writings explain the truth he illustrates in these stories, affirming the value of the material and the importance of the body. In *Mere Christianity* he says:

> Christianity is almost the only one of the great religions which thoroughly approves of the body—which believes that matter is good, that God Himself once took on a human body, that some kind of body is going to be given to us even in Heaven and is going to be an essential part of our happiness, our beauty, and our energy.[11]

The final pages of *The Last Battle* show that the entire physical universe, including the human body, will be redeemed and restored to its original splendor. We will look more closely at this idea in the chapter on heaven, but I will borrow from that chapter now to say that the Narnian heaven is a place of solid matter filled with hills and streams and trees, reflecting Lewis's conviction as to the nature of heaven. We will not be bodiless spirits but solid beings with bodies restored to supreme health and beauty. Lewis was convinced that when God created the material universe, he meant it to stay exactly as he made it. Satan came along and messed things up, but God has no intention of allowing him to ruin what he created and pronounced to be good.

Over and over Narnia lavishly affirms the goodness of the physical creation, showing characters delighting in the land's breathtaking beauty. A fine example occurs in *The Magician's Nephew*, when Digory and Polly, on the back of the flying horse Fledge, view the glory of the fresh Narnian world. As they descend into a green valley nestled in the heart of the mountains, the children hear "the chatter of the river on its stony bed and the creaking of trees in the light wind. A warm, good smell of sun-baked earth and grass and flowers came up to them." Snowy heights tower above the children, "one of them looking rose-red in the reflections of the sunset." As they continue their journey, they are awe-struck by the magnificent panorama below: "The valleys, far beneath them, were so green, and all the streams which tumbled down from the glaciers into the main river were so blue, that it was like flying over gigantic pieces of jewelry."[12] It's enough to send us looking for a wardrobe to scramble into.

But you don't have to go to Narnia to experience these wonders. In these descriptions Lewis opens our eyes to the beauty and glory of our own world. You can't go to Narnia, but Narnia's magic can come to you. When we look at our own earth, its streams and hills and foliage, its creatures, and even at each other, our vision is too easily fogged by the effects of the disaster that blighted the earth soon after creation. We tend to see less of the beauty and more of the damage. But Narnia helps us to penetrate the fog. In its newly created pristine mountains, streams, and graceful and noble creatures, we see the truth about our own creation. It also is a grand and glorious wonder. We bring the wonder of Narnia back to our own world, and our reopened eyes begin to see beyond the damage and perceive the glow of magic all around us. The visible wonder of the Narnian world reawakens the hidden wonder of our own.

INCURABLE ROMANTICS?

Young children find the whole world a romantic and fantastic place full of glory and wonder. Nothing is common to them; everything is extraordinary. It's when we grow older and begin to transform into muggles that we need tales of the fantastic to recall us to the truth. As Chesterton says, "These tales say that apples were golden only to refresh the forgotten moment when we found that they were green. They make rivers run with wine only to make us remember, for one wild moment, that they run with water."[13] In Narnia we recover the wonder at creation that we had in childhood. We find in Aslan's country the glory, the grandeur, the power, and the joy that lies inherent in reality. We bring it back to our own world and see all creation with new eyes. In some ways we should never grow up.

In *Prince Caspian* a forest of walking trees moves toward Aslan to join his march against the Telmarines. At first Susan and Lucy see the trees merely as a dark, unidentified mass, then as rising waves, then as woods on the move. As the trees draw near to Aslan, Lucy sees them as a crowd of treelike human shapes—birch-girls, willow-women, queenly beeches, shaggy oak-men, and other tree people bowing and shouting to Aslan. The presence of the Lion enables Lucy to see past the surface appearance into the soul of the trees. She sees the truth about them.

In seeing creation in its relationship to God, we see beneath the surface to the soul of it; its wonder and beauty become a powerful reality. The muggles that surround us will disdain that vision, accusing us of being incurable romantics looking at the world through rose-tinted glasses. "It's a jungle out there," they say, "a treacherous, messed-up world, a vale of tears, an arena of struggle for survival, and to see things otherwise is simply not facing up to reality." But the Christian sees everything through a new set of lenses—not rose tinted but polarized. Rather than coloring reality with an artificial hue, the Christian lens filters out the glare and shows it with new clarity. We see the solid truth about creation—the original steel beneath the coating of rust. The rust is not the truth about the metal; it is a blight that obscures the truth.

Beneath the damage, creation retains the good that God originally infused into it. That is why he has gone to such lengths to redeem and restore it. In spite of our sin and failure to be what he intended, he still places the high value on us that he pronounced on the day man and woman were first made. It is hard for us to fathom just how dearly he values us. In an address on the subject, Lewis said that as creations in the likeness of God we carry an unfathomable weight of glory, a glory latent within each of us that will shine forth when all things are restored. If we could see that glory now, it would forever alter the way we treat one another. He said:

> It is a serious thing to live in the society of possible gods and goddesses, to remember that the dullest and most uninteresting person you can talk to may one day be a creature which, if you saw it now, you would be strongly tempted to worship. . . . There are no ordinary people. You have never talked to a mere mortal. Nations, cultures, arts, civilisations—these are mortal, and their life is to ours as the life of a gnat.[14]

Our duty to our neighbors, our charge to be stewards of creation and to care for one another—these take on a larger meaning when we come to see the original glory that emanates from every created thing, including each one of us. Narnia leads us to put on those polarizing lenses, filtering out the glare and enabling us to see more clearly now the glory that was infused at creation and will be restored in redemption.

CHAPTER 3

MAMMALS, MOUNTAINS, AND MUFFINS

The Pleasures and Wonders of Creation

Narnia of the heathery mountains and the thymy downs,
Narnia of the many rivers, the plashing glens, the mossy caverns
and the deep forests ringing with the hammers of the Dwarfs.
Oh the sweet air of Narnia! An hour's life there is better than a
thousand years in Calormen.

—BREE, *THE HORSE AND HIS BOY*

That moment in *The Lion, the Witch and the Wardrobe* when Lucy first enters the home of the faun Tumnus is when most of us fall in love with Narnia. Like Lucy, we delight in the warmth and coziness of the place—a clean little cave with a carpeted floor, a table and two chairs, a dresser, a mantelpiece over a warm fire, a picture of an old faun over the mantel, and a shelf full of books. The faun serves Lucy tea (ah, these English authors!), which is not merely a drink but includes a brown egg, sardines on toast, buttered toast, toast with honey, and sugar-topped cake. We settle into the chair with Lucy, relishing the pleasures of warm hearth, tasty foods, exhilarating aromas, good companionship, and appealing sounds and textures.

And these pleasures—along with others that we will explore in this chapter—never cease as you go deeper into Narnia. Over and over Lewis charms us with such scenes of homey, simple pleasures as if he thinks this kind of thing is highly important. A few examples will give you the idea. In *The Horse and His Boy* the exhausted young hero Shasta is taken into a cave of kindly dwarfs and fed breakfast. Lewis spends a page and a half describing the menu (bacon, eggs, mushrooms, toast, butter, porridge, cream, coffee, hot milk), the aromas of the frying foods, the camaraderie, bustle, and hospitality of the dwarfs, and the inviting hominess of the cave (wood-lined walls, red-and-white checked tablecloth, a cuckoo clock, white curtains, and thick-paned windows). In *Prince Caspian* Lewis spends two pages telling us of a victory celebration including a bonfire, exuberant dances, elaborate feasting, and finally a contented sleep in the presence of friends and good company. On board the *Dawn Treader,* Lucy delights in waking up each morning to the reflections of the sunlit waves dancing on the ceiling of her cabin. She loves the bright blue sea, breathing the ocean air, and the shipboard breakfasts. As the magician's nephew Digory bathes in a mountain stream, Lewis asks us, "Have you ever bathed in a mountain river that is running in shallow cataracts over red and blue and yellow stones with the sun on it? It is as good as the sea: in some ways almost better."[1] After escaping from Underland, in *The Silver Chair,* Jill awakens from a snug sleep in a dwarf's cave. The soft, heather bed, the furry blanket, beams of morning sunlight, and the happy sounds and delicious aromas of breakfast delight her senses.

We tend to think of pleasure as oases of enjoyment in a desert of humdrum. But Narnia shows us that pleasure saturates all of life. There's pleasure for the taking not only in the spectacular events and activities—gourmet feasts, high achievements, great art and music, scintillating company, or rapturous lovemaking—it's available everywhere. Walking barefoot across the grass, a warm bath, a bowl of popcorn, a comfortable chair and a good book, a hot cup of coffee, a cat curled on a lap, dinner with your family, warm covers on a cold night—all creation is infused with delight that tells us something of the love of the God who created us to experience pleasure. Just wake up your senses and enjoy.

THE NARNIAN MENAGERIE

For many of us Narnia's greatest delight is its animals. Why did Lewis fill these stories with animals? For starters, he loved animals. As a child he filled his imaginary land of Boxen with them. He enjoyed the world of Kenneth Grahame's *The Wind in the Willows*, which certainly influenced Narnia. Often his letters to children spoke of birds, mice, cats, dogs, and rabbits he encountered about his house and garden. And in Narnia he no doubt indulged these likes, knowing that children—and most adults—love animals. We enjoy cuddling the soft fur of kittens and puppies just as Lucy longs to cuddle the mouse Reepicheep on the *Dawn Treader*. Furry creatures delight us, not only by the feel of their fur and the liquidity of their eyes, but by their playfulness, loyalty, beauty, and affection.

Lewis also understood that certain animals have characteristics that make them charming parodies of human qualities. Of Kenneth Grahame's choice of a toad as a principal character, Lewis says,

> The choice is based on the fact that the real toad's face has a grotesque resemblance to a certain kind of human face—a rather apoplectic face with a fatuous grin on it. . . . Looking at the creature we thus see, isolated and fixed, an aspect of human vanity in its funniest and most pardonable form.[2]

The expression of the owl suggests wisdom, thus the owls in *The Silver Chair* hold a parliament to advise Eustace and Jill. The quick, jerky movements of a squirrel suggest a certain type of nervous, energetic human personality parodied by Pattertwig in *Prince Caspian*. Lewis employed much of this kind of animal parody in Narnia, reviving in us the delight of sharing our world with God's creatures.

The Grandeur in Nature

Not only do the Narnia stories revel in the simple pleasures of the senses, they also present another kind of pleasure, something more like a thrill or a sense of being lifted and transported—a pleasure that draws us outside ourselves and makes our breath come deeper and our hearts beat faster. This feeling is similar to awe and evokes undefined longings.

In Narnia we often encounter this grand and exhilarating pleasure in Lewis's descriptions of nature. One example, previously mentioned, is in *The Magician's Nephew*, where Digory and Polly approach the Western Wild on the back of the flying horse. The rising sun illuminates a grand vista of high, snowy mountains surrounding them and glacier-fed streams tumbling into a jewellike blue river. A heavenly fragrance, warm and golden, rises up to them from juicy fruits and aromatic flowers. The children and readers alike find their spirits lifted by the magnificent panorama. Another example is the moment when the voyagers on the *Dawn Treader* approach the end of the world and see a brightness on the sea's horizon. It turns out to be a vast expanse of white lilies, stretching forward as far as they can see. The ship enters this Silver Sea and sails through it for several days.

> Day after day from all those miles and leagues of flowers there rose a smell which Lucy found it very hard to describe; sweet—yes, but not at all sleepy or overpowering, a fresh, wild, lonely smell that seemed to get into your brain and make you feel that you could go up mountains at a run or wrestle with an elephant.

She says to Caspian, "I feel that I can't stand much more of this, yet I don't want it to stop."[3] In Narnia we encounter the grand and majestic glory of nature as well as the homey and cozy.

The Truth behind Nature

This pleasure seen and experienced in nature—the grand vistas, towering mountains, majestic waterfalls, monumental clouds, and mist-shrouded forests—evokes dreams and inspirations and longings hard to explain or even identify. They inspire in almost all of us feelings of grandeur, sublimity, upward aspiration, and nobility.

Do these momentous sensations have any real significance? Or are they merely subjective personal feelings that don't really mean anything? Unbelievers do not grant any real meaning to the idea of majesty in a mountain or sublimity in a waterfall. They see mountains and waterfalls simply as natural phenomena caused by random convulsions of the earth, and the majesty and sublimity we attribute to them as nothing more than our feelings imposed on them. Lewis believed otherwise. In *The Abolition of Man* he reasons that unless there is such a thing as objective value—something inherently majestic about the mountain and sublime in the waterfall—such feelings are absurd, and the fact that all humans experience them is inexplicable.[4]

The mountain and the waterfall must possess some characteristic that is truly majestic or sublime, or they would not so consistently evoke such feelings in us. We have these sensations because mountains and waterfalls tell us something real and true. They shout that beauty, majesty, and grandeur are not empty feelings but real qualities that exist as firm realities. That's what Narnia is telling us. That breathlessness you experience when you first round the bend of the trail and see the towering mountain—an emotion of upward aspiration that stirs longings for you know not what—hints at something real and true. What is it that you long for at that moment? Obviously you don't desire the mountain itself; what would you do with a mountain? You sense that the mountain reminds you of something else, though you have nothing in your memory that matches the reminder. You might say it reminds you of something you have not yet experienced but sense that you are meant to experience. The beauty of the mountain is telling you that a greater beauty exists above it. The mountain is only an image—a shadow—pointing to that greater reality. That greater reality is the true reality that is the source of all beauty and the spring of all joy and delight that spills over into nature. That reality is God himself.

In *Prince Caspian* Lucy awakens one night feeling that a familiar voice has called her. She wanders among the trees, sensing life within them as if they are enchanted. But she is only half interested in the trees themselves. "She wanted to get beyond them to something else; it was from beyond them that the dear voice had called."[5] She hears within nature that voice calling from beyond nature. She wanders among the trees in search of what is beyond—"the dear voice that called." The voice of course is Aslan. Lucy senses in the beauty of the natural world the supernatural reality that exists beyond it. She sees the truth behind nature as the God who loves her, and she willingly goes through nature to find him. In Narnia the voice of nature is an echo of the voice of God drawing us toward our true home.

When Jewel the unicorn in *The Last Battle* reaches the Narnian heaven, he says, "I have come home at last! This is my real country! I belong here. This is the land I have been looking for all my life, though I never knew it till now." He says he loved the old Narnia, because "it sometimes looked a little like this."[6] Earthly beauty is not to be shunned as a temptation but enjoyed as a first glimpse of the unbounded heavenly delights that await us in God's true country.

MISJUDGING THE PHYSICAL

Do you find it surprising that stories so renowned for their spiritual insight contain so much emphasis on the sensual delights of the material creation? Many Christians don't trust sensual delight. They equate *sensual* with *sinful* and fear that the pleasure of the senses will draw them away from their focus on the spiritual. Influenced by ancient heresies that will not die, they see a great divide between the spiritual and physical, with the spiritual the higher value and the physical the lower. They believe that in our central essence we humans are spirits. We are trapped in bodies, which will eventually be discarded, allowing us to exist in pure spirit form freed from the contamination of the sensual.

Lewis believed otherwise. He saw a physical body as essential to our humanity, not only here on earth, but in heaven as well. Narnia demonstrates vividly his conviction that our bodies are designed to experience the sensual delights of nature. One of his letters to Malcolm explains why:

> But for our body one whole realm of God's glory—all that we receive through the senses—would go unpraised. . . . I fancy the "beauties of nature" are a secret God has shared with us alone. That may be one of the reasons why we were made— and why the resurrection of the body is an important doctrine.[7]

Far from believing the body to be the evil side of humanity, he was convinced that our souls lead our bodies into most of our sins. "Bless the body," he wrote. "Mine has led me into many scrapes, but I've led it into far more. If the imagination were obedient, the appetites would give us very little trouble."[8] The body is not evil; it was pronounced good on the day God made it.

To be truly human is to be physical as well as spiritual. A human spirit without a body is useless. Our spirits must have a way of expressing themselves and performing what they will to do, and our bodies provide the necessary apparatus. Visiting the sick, teaching the gospel, and feeding the hungry all are spiritual activities, but a spirit can perform none of them without a body. The body is crucial to our being.

When God created Adam and Eve, the fusion of spirit and body was meant to be permanent. This is affirmed in the great lengths to which Jesus has gone to redeem the body. Death is not a way of getting rid of the physical body so we can be purely spiritual. Death is an interruption to God's intent—a way of getting rid of the infection of sin that ravages our bodies so they can be renovated to the purity and perfection he originally intended. The idea is not to destroy the body permanently but to bring it back in its right form. The apostle Paul put it this way: "For the trumpet will sound, and the dead will be raised incorruptible, and we shall be changed. For this corruptible must put on incorruption, and this mortal must put on immortality."[9]

Jesus' resurrected body demonstrated the kind of body that awaits us—fully physical with all the effects of the Fall removed. His new body had "put on immortality" and was now death-proof and age-proof. Because God in his goodness will not allow evil to ruin what he created to be good, our bodies are to be redeemed from the ravages of corruption. Our redeemed bodies will not be wispy or less than substantial as we imagine ghosts to be; they will be completely physical—more solid and substantial than they are now. They will be "spiritual bodies" in the sense that they will be immune to death and corruption and happily submitted to God.

This redemption of the physical applies to all material nature as well. Our bodies are part of the larger package that includes the entire physical universe. Paul tells us that along with our redemption "the creation itself also will be delivered from the bondage of corruption into the glorious liberty of the children of God."[10] The destruction of the heavens and the earth in the book of Revelation will not remove the physical creation from the universe forever. It's the kind of thing a landscaper does to a lawn in the spring. He burns it away so that the new growth will be free of all the fungi, moss, parasites, and matted dead grass within it.

Narnia shows us the truth of the Bible: The physical creation is neither evil nor expendable. The whole of it is supremely good and will be redeemed. The Narnian heaven is the original Narnian creation renovated and enhanced. In the new heavenly Narnia, King Tirian of *The Last Battle* remembers the smell of bread and milk at suppertime when he was a child. The entire country reminds him and his companions of holidays and good memories, and each new vista is a wonder of breathtaking beauty. The whole picture is a resounding affirmation of earthly beauty and our pleasure in it. Even the simple pleasures will not be lost in heaven; they will be restored.

DESIGNED FOR PLEASURE

Is it possible to look at the flash of a lightning bug, the suit of a penguin, the beak of a pelican, the pouch of a kangaroo, the cavorting of a dolphin, or the smile of a beautiful girl and not wonder what God was thinking when he made that? Narnia shows us what God was thinking: *Those humans of mine are going to love this.* Narnia shows us an altogether different God than we find in many churches where any sense of joy is buried beneath "all that regimen of tiptoe tread and lowered voice—which the word 'religion' suggests to so many people now."[11]

Narnia shows God shouting through nature to tell us how deeply he loves us. The stories help us develop sensitivity to the language of nature so that we can hear his voice and feel the loving beat of his heart. Everything about the material creation reflects God's intention that we delight in our existence. We are designed for pleasure. Our bodies are loaded with sensors capable of experiencing delight in the world and in one another, and God meant us to enjoy it all.

After the defeat of the Telmarines in *Prince Caspian*, Aslan leads the victorious Narnians on a joyous march (or is it more of a dance?) to the town of Beruna. Along the way nature flourishes again where it has been abused, with vines springing up everywhere. And many people who have been burdened with gray, prosaic lives catch the spirit and join the march. They are attracted to Aslan because of the joy he brings, not because of a need to conform to some pious ideal about reverence and austere decorum in the presence of Deity. Narnia reveals the side of God we seldom find behind stained glass or hear from the pulpits or see in religious art—a God with a smile on his face and a twinkle in his eye who wants nothing more than for his creatures to experience delight. A God of extreme, extravagant, lavish, abounding *goodness*. And it rushes in on us from all crea-tion—sounds, smells, sights, tastes, and textures—all made for our enjoyment. And he gave us five delightable senses just so we could revel in these experiences.

And through these experiences come to know him.

CHAPTER 4

BAD MAGIC

The Invasion of Evil

*You must learn, child, that what would be wrong for you or for
any of the common people is not wrong in a great Queen such
as I. . . . We must be freed from all rules.*

—JADIS THE WITCH, *THE MAGICIAN'S NEPHEW*

If Aslan created Narnia as a bright and beautiful world of perpetual glory and delight, why does Lucy find it frozen in perpetual winter? What went wrong? How could evil ever get into a place like Narnia?

In *The Magician's Nephew* we learn the answer. A selfish amateur magician, Andrew Ketterley, dupes his nephew Digory and the boy's friend Polly into testing a set of magical rings that he is too cowardly to test himself. The rings draw the children into an alternate dimension and eventually to a city silent and empty except for massive ruins of ancient buildings. As they enter one of the ruins, they come upon a sight so eerie that it makes their hearts stop. The room is filled with hundreds of seated people, dressed in finery and silent and still as wax figures. One figure, a woman, is beautiful and extremely tall. Her clothing is regal, and her face bears a look of proud fierceness. In the center of the room, on a four-foot pillar, hangs a little golden bell with a hammer beside it. These words are engraved on the pillar:

Make your choice, adventurous Stranger;
Strike the bell and bide the danger,
Or wonder, till it drives you mad,
What would have followed if you had.[1]

You can imagine how difficult it would be to resist striking that bell. And of course Digory cannot resist. The sound awakens the beautiful giantess from a deep enchantment. She tells them she is Jadis, the last queen of Charn, who destroyed her world with evil spells rather than let her sister rule it. Though the children try to escape her, she manages to accompany them back to London. When she causes a riot, they use the magic rings to get her out of London and into another world.

The world they enter is Narnia, where, as we have already noted, creation is in progress. Jadis tries to disable Aslan by hurling at him an iron bar she wrenched from a London lamppost. When the bar bounces off the Lion unnoticed, she shrieks with rage, realizing she has encountered a being she cannot conquer. She flees into the wilds of Narnia.

Aslan tells the newly created rational animals that they must take steps to keep Narnia safe. "For though the world is not five hours old an evil has already entered it."[2] Throughout the rest of the *Chronicles,* we find the effects of evil—bad magic. A bleak winter grips the land for a hundred years. A rightful king is murdered and his son deposed. A wicked witch turns innocent creatures to stone. The country suffers attacks from its Calormene enemies. A prince and thousands of creatures endure slavery in underground caverns. All creatures suffer pain and death, and they contend with selfishness, conspiracy, tyranny, cruelty, deceit, disease, decay, and all the other horrors that evil inflicts.

EVIL IN OUR WORLD

In our own world a similar thing happened. Everything was created pristine and perfect. All nature was in harmony and free from pain and decay. The first man and woman were perfect in body and spirit, harboring no evil thoughts. They were in perfect harmony and joyful companionship with nature, each other, and God, who spoke with them face to face as a dear friend. Evil did not exist in our world and could not enter it unless this couple rejected God.

That rejection came about in this way: God gave them the fruit of all the trees on earth for food, but he pointed out one tree in the center of their garden and told them not to eat of it because it would bring death. A subversive enemy, whom most Christians believe to be an angel driven from heaven in a rebellion against God, entered the garden in the guise of a beautiful serpent (even snakes were appealing then). He deceived the couple into eating the forbidden fruit.

That act showed God that the man and woman had chosen to expel him from their lives and follow their own notions of right and wrong. So he honored their choice. He withdrew from them and left them on their own. The result was utter disaster. The world was designed to function with man and woman as rulers under God, but without God, they were incapable of handling the job. The enemy Satan seized his opportunity to move in and take over. He made himself lord of the earth, and all creation went haywire. Evil, death, decay, strife, disease, pain, disaster, and tragedy blighted all the good in nature. The man and woman now had to labor to exhaustion to eke out a living from the ground. Though they were created to live forever, they found their health, strength, and beauty leeched away until they wore down and died. This tragic event—the entry of evil when man and woman turned from God to themselves—is known as the Fall.

The entry of evil into Narnia illuminates the Fall of humanity in several significant ways. Digory's curiosity draws him to strike the bell in Charn. I cannot but imagine that Eve felt the same kind of curiosity about the forbidden fruit. It seems to be in our nature: The thing forbidden becomes the thing desired. We've got to have it. We must try it. When we see a "wet paint" sign, why do we feel the urge to touch the paint? Imagine moving into a new house and finding in a dark closet a red button set in a metal plate on the wall engraved with the words "Do not press this button." How long do you think that button would remain untouched? That is the nature of the temptation that Digory faced, and it must have been similar for Eve. The Genesis story has her succumbing to the urging of Satan with little dialogue and little resistance. The account may be a simplification of what really happened; on the other hand, Eve may have needed little urging. She may have been waiting for an excuse to pluck that fruit.

Yet burning curiosity is no excuse. When called to account before Aslan for awakening the witch and bringing her into Narnia, Digory tries to justify his action. He admits to striking the bell, but says he thinks he "was a bit enchanted by the writing" under it. "Do you?" Aslan asks pointedly. Before the face of the Lion, all excuses wither and nothing but truth will do. "No," says Digory. "I see now I wasn't. I was only pretending."[3]

Digory standing before Aslan reflects a similar scene in the Bible when Adam and Eve stand before God to account for eating the forbidden fruit. "That woman made me do it," complains Adam. "The devil made me do it," responds Eve. But the excuses don't wash. God holds them responsible for their act and pronounces their self-imposed doom. They have alienated themselves from God, and they will die. Nature will run amok, and the world will become infested with pain and disaster. No matter how hard it may be to resist the temptation, no matter how extenuating the circumstance, God holds them responsible for the choice they made, and they must live with the results of it.

THE GREAT COMPLIMENT

Why did Aslan allow evil to enter Narnia? Why didn't he banish the witch before she could work her bad magic?

You may ask the same question about our world. God knew that

Satan had infiltrated Eden. He knew that his happy and perfect couple and their magnificent world were at risk. Why didn't he banish that conniving snake? Surprisingly we find the answer in the high compliment God has paid to humanity. When we read in Genesis that God created the species man in his own image, we hardly comprehend the magnitude of that statement. God is the prime mover of this and all other universes. We were created to be what you might call "deputy gods" on this earth. We were created in his image so that our every act would reflect to all creation his likeness. We were created to be dynamic agents of his power, creativity, wisdom, and love. As Lewis notes, "Every Christian is to become a little Christ."[4]

As if all that were not enough, God added to it the greatest compliment he could give a creature: free will. Why did God trust man and woman with free will when the misuse of it would ruin his world? If all he wanted was something on earth to run things for him, he could have designed robots or automatons as NASA engineers design such devices to perform planetary probes. Lewis answered the question in *Mere Christianity*:

> Because free will, though it makes evil possible, is also the only thing that makes possible any love or goodness or joy worth having. . . . The happiness which God designs for His higher creatures is the happiness of being freely, voluntarily united to Him and to each other in an ecstasy of love and delight. . . . And for that they must be free.[5]

When God created man and woman, he wanted something more than just machines controlled by signals or another animal controlled by instinct. He wanted a creature that could love. Love compelled is not love at all. Authentic love is a free choice. God allows us to choose whether or not we will love him and do his will. That is the compliment. That is the ultimate stroke of godlikeness that we possess. We are free to make decisions that have a real effect on life both here and now and also in eternity. We are, to use Tolkien's term, "subcreators," free to make and move and shape things according to our desires. When God made man and woman the rulers of the earth, it was more than a mere title; he was placing in our hands a power with enormous implication.

Now we can see why God did not bar Satan from Eden or remove the dangerous and provocative tree from the garden. The man and woman had to be free to choose, and to remove the option to sin would destroy the choice. Options must exist for freedom to have meaning. Adam and Eve chose wrongly, but God had to let their choice stand. Had he stepped in and corrected the couple's mistake, their freedom would have been meaningless. The compliment of freedom would have been rescinded and our actions would have no real meaning. What we choose to do would have no effect on the world or its future.

The inaction of Aslan in not deporting the witch pictures the profound restraint of Deity. In Narnia as on the earth, free will means making free choices. Free will brought evil into Narnia, and in the name of freedom, evil must remain.

Unmasking Evil

Evil often masquerades as good or blurs the lines between good and evil, making it hard to discern the difference. Narnia cuts through the ambiguity and exposes evil for what it is. Let's explore several characteristics of evil, both petty and deadly, that show up in these stories.

Evil is self-destructive. In Narnia we see the self-destructive nature of evil when the witch Jadis explains to the children why she destroyed Charn. Her sister was queen, but Jadis wanted the throne for herself. Jadis declared war on her sister, but when she saw defeat looming, she uttered the Deplorable Word, a spell that killed every living thing in Charn except for Jadis herself. In *The Silver Chair* the queen of the Underland does a similar thing. She sets a spell to

destroy all her realm if ever she is killed. It's rule or ruin. If I can't
have it, I will destroy it.

The central characteristic of evil is destruction. Good creates
and brings order; evil destroys and brings chaos. The paradox of evil
is that it ultimately destroys itself. When the cancer succeeds in
devouring the patient, the cancer also dies for lack of anything to
feed on. We can rightly say that evil is *consumed* with destruction,
and the double meaning applies in both senses. Evil is so fixated on
destroying that it cannot stop until it destroys itself. We see this principle in operation when Jesus exorcises a mass of demons from a pos-
sessed man. The demons can't stand to be disembodied and beg him
to send them into a nearby herd of swine. Jesus complies, and when
the demons enter the swine, they drive them to suicide in the sea,
thus destroying their own hosts.[6]

Evil is cowardly and self-centered. Narnia displays this facet of
evil in Digory's uncle Andrew. He will not take the risk of going into
an unknown parallel dimension to satisfy his own lust for knowledge.
Instead he manipulates the children into going, exposing them to
great danger. He has used up much of Aunt Letty's savings under the
guise of managing it for her, while not working at all himself. Thrust
into Narnia against his will, Andrew calls Digory naughty and imper-
tinent for refusing to slip away and leave the others stranded in the
empty, uncreated world. When he sees Digory bravely approaching
the Lion to ask for a silver apple to save Digory's mother, Andrew
angrily calls him back so he can get the rings for himself and return
to safety in London.

Evil does not know itself to be evil. When Prince Rilian of Narnia
lives under the spell of the Green Lady, he is insensitive to the evil
she plans, caring nothing for the innocent people she intends to conquer and enslave. He has lost all empathy and love, though he is
unaware of the loss. But for one hour each night, the lady has Rilian
tied to the silver chair to protect him from what she calls his nightly
"enchantment." During this hour he remembers the fair images of

Narnia. He remembers truth and love and justice. For this one hour Rilian is actually freed from his real enchantment—the influence of evil. He also knows who he is. He says, "Now that I am myself I can remember that enchanted life, though while I was enchanted I could not remember my true self."[7] Good knows evil, but evil knows neither good nor itself.

This principle explains our vulnerability to the slippery slope of encroaching evil. Like the heat of the stove increasing so slowly that the frog in the kettle does not feel it, evil numbs us as it intensifies. Movies and TV shows that appalled us ten years ago are now standard fare. Standards for sexual morality thought absolute by our parents seem overly restrictive to the present generation.

Our tendency toward self-justification is evidence that evil does not know itself. I see the wrong in others clearly but not the wrong in myself. We condemn actions of others that we allow for ourselves because we have good reasons for doing them or because their excess exceeds ours. The driver speeding at seventy-five miles per hour condemns the scofflaw hurling down the road at eighty. The person who is twenty pounds overweight condemns as a glutton the person who is fifty pounds over. The driver in front of me poking along in the neighborhood at ten miles per hour is a hazard to safety. But when I creep through a strange suburb looking for an address, those people honking behind me ought to understand and cut me some slack.

The witch Jadis did not see herself as evil. She thought herself above the law on the grounds that a great queen ought to be free from the rules that bind common people. We've seen the same thing in our presidents, CEOs, entertainment personalities, and sports figures. And we usually don't have to look too deep to find it in ourselves.

Evil hates good and often characterizes it as evil. Both Jadis and Andrew hate the voice of Aslan as he sings the creation song. Jadis hates it because she realizes Aslan's magic is more powerful than hers. Evil fears and hates anything stronger than itself for it feels its self-centeredness threatened. Good, simply by being good, judges evil to be wrong.

Those committed to evil cannot allow anyone to recognize that good is right; they must redefine good as evil to justify striking back at it.

BEARING EVIL, SHARING GOOD

As it did in Narnia, the bad magic of evil has brought sorrow, pain, tragedy, and death alongside the unbounded delight and joy God intended for us. In spite of it all, we still retain that compliment of free will. The Fall doesn't diminish our freedom to act; we are still movers and shakers, and we can choose which way we move and shake. We can make the world around us better or worse. We cannot undo the effects of the Fall, but we can ease and even reverse some of them. We can be selfless in the face of selfishness, show love in the face of hate, and give to those who have need. Although the Fall brought evil into a world of good, we can now bring good back into a world of evil by submitting to the Spirit of God and taking his will into every situation. We can still perform as the "deputy gods" we were created to be.

The good in creation is still intact, still a source of delight. But now it is sometimes necessary to deny ourselves some of that good and willingly take on some of the pain. In a world filled with both good and evil, we must love our neighbors enough to share both their joys and their sorrows. Take all the joy that comes your way and enjoy it, but not at the expense of those to whom it's denied. In those cases we take their pain and bear it with them, so that the bad magic of evil will be diminished by the good we bring to others.

CHAPTER 5

TURKISH DELIGHT
Temptation and Sin

He had eaten his share of the dinner, but he hadn't really enjoyed it because he was thinking all the time about Turkish Delight—and there's nothing that spoils the taste of good ordinary food half so much as the memory of bad magic food.

—THE LION, THE WITCH AND THE WARDROBE

⸺ ◆◆◆ ⸺

The White Witch knows how to destroy an enemy: discover his secret weakness—what he can't resist—and give him a taste of it. When it's gone, he will crave more, and next time even more yet, until he gorges himself to death. It works in Narnia, and it works in our world.

How did she learn such cunning? In the days after the creation of Narnia, far away in the uninhabited wilds in the north, the witch is known as Jadis, and she burns with hatred for the Lion. She steals silver apples from the magical tree, which lengthens her life to many hundreds of years. But they are not happy years. She broods and increases her skill in dark magic until the day she can return to Narnia and wrest it from the Lion. When *The Lion, the Witch and the Wardrobe* opens, her conquest has already occurred. She is now the White Witch, and she holds the land in the icy grip of perpetual winter.

She knows of the prophecy predicting her end—when four

children sit on the four thrones at the Narnian castle of Cair Paravel. So she keeps a sharp lookout for invaders and coerces her subjects into informing her if any sons of Adam or daughters of Eve ever appear in Narnia.

When Edmund secretly follows Lucy through the wardrobe, the witch finds him alone and grills him curtly until she discovers that he is human. She then turns sweet and solicitous. She gives him a mantle against the cold, takes him onto her sleigh, and produces his favorite sweet treat, Turkish delight. Edmund greedily stuffs himself with the candy while the witch questions him and learns of his brother and two sisters. After eating the treat, he wants more, though he dares not ask for it. But the witch knows quite well what he is thinking. She also knows that this is enchanted Turkish delight, "and that anyone who had once tasted it would want more and more of it, and would even, if they were allowed, go on eating it till they killed themselves."[1]

Here we have a clear illustration of the nature of temptation and the result of yielding to it. Sin is like an addiction. The allure of it leads to the taste; the taste leads to lust for more; and the lust for more leads to fatal excess. As the church leader James wrote, "Temptation comes from the lure of our own evil desires. These evil desires lead to evil actions, and evil actions lead to death."[2] We go on grasping for our favorite pleasure even when it becomes no longer pleasurable but destructive. It enslaves the will, becoming almost impossible to resist until it closes in for the kill.

The White Witch promises Edmund more Turkish delight if he will bring his brother and two sisters to her. She explains that she wants to make him the prince of the country, and that his siblings are to be his courtiers and nobles. She promises that all his desires will be fulfilled if he will simply do as she asks. And he determines to do it, because he cannot resist the promise of more Turkish delight.

After succumbing to the White Witch's temptation, Edmund returns through the wardrobe to our world. Although he already is a bit of a bully, his faults are now intensified. He is snappish, surly, argumentative, and contrary. He even lies about having been in Narnia, causing the other children to doubt Lucy's claim that she has been to such a place. He is already on the side of the White Witch, ready to betray his family for more Turkish delight and power. Sin causes people to sacrifice all that is good to get the thing they crave.

Edmund is not the first human boy the White Witch has tempted. We learn in *The Magician's Nephew* that hundreds of years earlier when she went by the name Jadis, she met Digory Kirke at the tree of the silver apples in the garden of the northern wilds. Aslan had sent him on a quest for a silver apple. He was to take only one and bring it to the Lion intact. After Digory plucked the apple, the witch urged him to eat it himself. She told him it would give him eternal life, youth, and knowledge that would make him happy all his life. He and she could be king and queen of the world. She cast doubt on Aslan's goodness, tempting the boy to think the Lion self-ish because he wanted the apple for himself.

The witch's temptation of both Digory and Edmund is the kind of thing that happened in the Garden of Eden in our world and is repeated in ordinary lives every day. All temptation and all sin display similar characteristics. The White Witch in Narnia uses the same tactics that Satan used in Eden when he said to Eve, "Has God indeed said, 'You shall not eat of every tree of the garden'?" (*He's holding back on you, woman.*) When Eve explains that God has for-bidden one tree because its fruit is deadly, Satan replies, "You will not surely die. For God knows that in the day you eat of it your eyes will be opened, and you will be like God, knowing good and evil." (*God has lied to you, lady. He's hiding something. This fruit will make you equal to him, and he doesn't want rivals. He wants to stay in charge and keep you under his thumb. He's looking out for his own good, not yours. This fruit will free you and give you wisdom equal to his, so you can get out on your own, be yourself, and do your own thing.*) "So when the woman saw that the tree was good for food, that it was pleasant to the eyes, and a tree desirable to make one wise, she took of its fruit and ate."[3] It looked good, it would make her feel good, and it would give her knowledge and power. She snatched it off the tree and stuffed it into her mouth.

Eve succumbed to the basic temptation that all her descendants have fallen for—what the apostle John summed up as all that keeps us from loving God, "the lust of the flesh, the lust of the eyes, and the pride of life."[4]

It's the same kind of temptation Satan applied to Christ in the desert. After fasting for forty days, Jesus was ravenously hungry. Satan came to him and urged him to turn stones into bread. When Jesus refused, Satan pressed him to show his faith in God by throwing himself off the temple pinnacle to see if God would save him. Jesus refused again. Then Satan took him to a high mountain and showed him all the kingdoms of the world; they would all be his if he would only turn his allegiance from God to Satan. Jesus refused emphatically and sent the devil packing.[5]

The temptation of Digory and Edmund in Narnia, as well as that of Eve and Christ in the real world, boils down the essence of all temptation, including that which you and I face every day. No matter the details and circumstance, Satan's message is the same: "Get out from under God's thumb; take charge of your own life. I can give you all you need, satisfy all your desires, and you can have it all now. No need to wait for God, who may or may not give what you want." Perhaps you've got a good shot at your lifelong ambition of being a company vice president, but it means hiding certain company activities from clients and auditors. Can God really expect anyone to turn down such a once-in-a-lifetime opportunity? After all, everyone hides some little something. And on your new salary you can triple your church contribution. Perhaps you're in love with the man in the next office, but he's married, though unhappily. Can God expect you to live a life of hopeless longing and loneliness, just because of the technicality of a mistaken wedding vow? Surely you have a right to happiness. Satan's message is that you should go for it. You can have what you want if you'll just put aside God's irksome rules. Take matters into your own hands and create your own destiny. The continual difficulty we encounter in resisting these temptations shows our fallenness and our addiction to sin.

EVIL DESIRES?

Because the Fall has weakened our wills, our desires are easily inflamed by temptation and seem to lead us into most of our troubles. This fact has led some religions to denounce all desire, claiming that the way to achieve peace is to reach a state in which we have absolutely no desire left. Then we will be exempt from temptation and free of the effects of evil.

But of course we will also be free of all joy. Yes, our desires do lead us into trouble, but they also lead us into joy. Christianity teaches that desire is a good thing. The ultimate object behind all desires is God, and our desires were given to lead us ultimately to him. Desires are not to be renounced but fulfilled. They are not to be suppressed but directed through their proper objects—the good gifts God has placed in creation—to God himself. These gifts are beams from his glory. Each of them reflects something about his nature. Our joy is to travel up those beams and experience God himself. As Lewis says of that central desire for God:

> Earthly pleasures were never meant to satisfy it, but only to arouse it, to suggest the real thing. If that is so, I must take care, on the one hand, never to despise, or be unthankful for, these earthly blessings, and on the other, never to mistake them for the something else of which they are only a kind of copy, or echo, or mirage.[6]

All desires are to be satisfied, but in their proper way, in their proper time, and by their proper object.

TEMPTATION AND EVIL

Notice that Narnia is created before evil comes on the scene. Things cannot work the other way around; evil cannot be created first with good coming in afterward. Evil cannot precede good, because evil cannot exist independent of good. Good, on the other hand, can exist independent of evil. Contrary to common thought, good and evil are not equal opposites; evil is a dependent parasite on good. Evil is to good not as black is to white but rather as rust is to metal, as disease is to health, and as death is to life. It can exist only where it can feed on good. We've already noted that the essence of evil is destruction. It eats away at good until the good is destroyed.

You can see that evil does not exist on its own in the fact that no one ever commits evil for its own sake. Edmund did not ask for Turkish delight because he wanted to be bad or to have a stomachache. He wanted the sweet taste of the treat. As Lewis explains, "You can be good for the mere sake of goodness: you cannot be bad for the mere sake of badness. . . . Badness cannot succeed even in being bad in the same way in which goodness is good. Goodness is, so to speak, itself: badness is only spoiled goodness."[7]

All who commit evil are grasping for some good, but they are trying to get at it in the wrong way, trying to get too much of it, hurting others in the process of getting it, or trying to get a good that belongs to someone else. Gluttons eat too much because they desire the good taste of food and the comfort of feeling filled. Tyrants grasp for power because they desire significance. Adulterers have sex because they desire its pleasurable sensations. Food, significance, and sex are all good things. There's nothing wrong with desiring them. One cannot desire anything intrinsically evil; such a thing does not exist, because God is the Creator of all, and he pronounced it all good. As

Lewis has the archdemon Screwtape say of God, "He made the pleasures: all our research so far has not enabled us to produce one. All we can do is to encourage the humans to take the pleasures which our Enemy has produced, at times, or in ways, or in degrees, which He has forbidden."[8] Lewis explains elsewhere, "And do you now begin to see why Christianity has always said that the devil is a fallen angel? That is not a mere story for the children. It is a real recognition of the fact that evil is a parasite, not an original thing."[9]

In an unfallen world we would freely enjoy all the good God intended for us without restriction, because our desires would be in balance with our needs and properly directed by God's Spirit toward their proper objects. But in a fallen world where desires turn selfish and run rampant, restrictions are necessary to prevent disaster. It's when we ignore the restrictions and go for the good in our own way that we commit evil.

The witch Jadis illustrates the point. The tree that grows in the wild heights of Narnia bears silver apples that give health, protection, and life to those who pluck them *at the right time and in the right way*. But as the Lion explains, the fruit does not work happily for anyone who plucks it at his or her own will. If any Narnian steals an apple unbidden, eating the fruit at the wrong time and in the wrong way, that creature will loathe it ever after and his or her days will be filled with misery.[10] Jadis desires long life. Nothing wrong with that. We all have a built-in desire for eternal existence. But eternal life is a gift that comes with desiring God, the eternal One. Jadis hates Aslan and refuses to depend on him for the eternal existence she craves, so she steals one of the apples. Though it gives her the thing she sought, she loathes the fruit afterward and cannot stand to come near it. She finds only misery in achieving her desire in the wrong, self-seeking way.

Had Jadis loved Aslan and desired eternal life because it would allow her to be with him forever, temptation to eat the fruit would have had no effect. Temptation works only when desire encounters restriction. There is no restriction to the experience of good when desire is fused with love for God, for he allows everything that brings us to real joy. It's because our desires have turned away from God to ourselves that we need restrictions on how we satisfy our desires for the good things in creation. When we yield to temptation and bypass the restrictions, the good turns sour.

So gluttony eventually flattens the pleasure of taste, but the glutton cannot stop overindulging even though it destroys his health. The tyrant seeking significance in power finds it meaningless when he achieves it and thus grasps for more. Adulterers find that guilt and deception tarnish the pleasure, and if they succeed in breaking up a marriage and wedding each other, the new marriage often sours with the same problems that caused them to divorce their previous spouses. Continual one-night stands mock the oneness everyone seeks in sex, and each act becomes increasingly meaningless. Often partners loathe each other after their lust is spent, as did King David's son Amnon after he raped his sister Tamar. The question, "But will you love me in the morning?" is a sort of standing joke because it expresses tacit recognition of the universal tendency of stolen pleasure to turn sour.

The tree of the silver apples in Narnia reminds us of a second tree that stood in the Garden of Eden. This tree—the Tree of Life— receives less attention than the infamous Tree of the Knowledge of Good and Evil, but it is no less significant. After Adam and Eve ate the forbidden fruit, God expelled them from Eden and posted an angelic guard to prevent them from eating of the Tree of Life and living forever.

It may appear that God was being cruel to this poor couple. It hardly seems fair that he would deny them access to the tree that could supply the antidote to the death they had just eaten. But God was actually performing a mercy. The fate of Jadis explains it all. Eating the silver apple gave her long life, but it was a life of misery filled with evil, hate, and insatiable lust for power. In a fallen world death is not merely a punishment; it is also a mercy, not only to Adam and Eve, but to you and me as well.

TEMPTATION OVERCOME

Edmund yielded to temptation and became entrapped by his craving for Turkish delight. Digory also yielded when he struck the bell in Charn and brought alive the evil that invaded Narnia. But toward the end of *The Magician's Nephew*, Digory makes a huge turnaround and resists an enormous temptation under difficult circumstances. Just as Jesus in the desert with Satan refuses to make bread for himself, Digory in the garden with Jadis refuses to take the apple for himself. Although he is greatly tempted, he follows Aslan's orders and brings the apple to him.

Sometimes we tend to think that temptation is simply too overpowering to resist. But it isn't. We can find the strength to resist it. Note that Digory has "outside help" in resisting the urgings of the witch. As he wrestles with the temptation to take an apple for himself, which he is forbidden to do, the urge seems irresistible until he looks up and sees in the tree a beautiful bird of paradise. He senses that this magical bird is watching him from above, and the thought dampens his urge to eat the fruit. But that is not his only deterrent. Digory has had principles such as "do not steal" drummed into his head by his parents, and their teaching rises to his conscience at the moment of temptation.

These kinds of deterrents do work. I don't know how many times I have refrained from sin because of the teaching of my parents or even because I didn't want to disappoint them. And later I often refrained because I wanted to be a model to my children and later to my grandchildren. All are watching. All would be affected or influenced by my failure. The eyes of others can be a helpful restraint holding us back from the magnetic pull of temptation.

Though these deterrents helped Digory resist the witch, they were not the central source of his strength. As the Lion gave him his charge, it "drew a deep breath, stooped its head even lower and gave him a Lion's kiss. And at once Digory felt that new strength and courage had gone into him."[11] Aslan gives Digory his own spirit. So armed, he has all the power he needs to make right choices. He has no excuse for failure. The God of Narnia himself has fortified his will.

Throughout the Narnian stories we find affirmation that human will is capable of making right choices. And here again we find a truth in Narnia that shows a truth about ourselves. We are given the freedom to choose and the ability to choose right. Hard as the choice may be, the responsibility for it is ours alone. We have that compliment of free will. We are decision makers—movers and shakers. Our wills, aligned with God, are capable of making the hard decision and resisting temptation.

The idea prevalent today is quite the opposite. We are conditioned to see ourselves as victims of our desires and accept little responsibility for managing our wills and resisting temptation. In such an atmosphere it's easy to feel justified in drifting with the stream. Schools give condoms to students because the wisdom of the day thinks it unrealistic to expect teens to abstain from sex. Those raging hormones will demand satisfaction, and mere will power cannot stand up to them. Overeaters sue restaurants for their own failure to control their weight, and careless people sue when they mishandle cups of hot coffee. It's everybody's fault but mine. We have become spineless victims of external circumstance, forfeiting our high position as movers and shakers in God's creation.

Narnia reminds us of the nobility we have as God's creatures by showing us that we bear responsibility for our own choices. Without that responsibility we are little more than amoebas bumping about aimlessly in response to random stimuli. Narnia illustrates the truth that permeates Scripture. Men and women are capable of making right choices, and when aligned with the power of God, no power in the universe can stand in their way.

But when you think on it, isn't that a wonderful gift? Doesn't it give you a sense of great worth to know that God gives you responsibility for your own choices? And that he loves you enough to give restrictions to guide you in making them? And not only that, he also gives his own Spirit to back up your right decisions, providing the power to resist when temptation attacks. That is an enormous gift. To know that you have that kind of strength, that kind of worth, and that kind of significance should give you chill bumps.

———•◆•———

CHAPTER 6

DEEP MAGIC
BEFORE TIME

The Defeat of Death

I have settled the matter. She has renounced the
claim on your brother's blood.

—ASLAN, THE LION, THE WITCH AND THE WARDROBE

In *The Lion, the Witch and the Wardrobe*, Edmund is in deep trouble. He faces a deadly dilemma that threatens his life—a dilemma exactly like one that you and I face. He foolishly believed the promises of the White Witch for unending Turkish delight and a throne from which he would rule over his brother and sisters if he would only bring them to her. When they decided to seek Aslan instead of following him to the witch's castle, Edmund went to her alone. But after the White Witch learned from Edmund where the other three children were heading, she enslaved him. And now she plans to execute him to keep the prophecy of the four thrones from being fulfilled. That prophecy predicts the end of her reign when four sons of Adam and daughters of Eve sit on thrones of Narnia.

While the White Witch is sharpening her knife for the execution, Aslan's forces rescue Edmund. But the rescue proves meaningless when she reminds the Lion of the "Deep Magic from the Dawn of Time" written on the scepter of the Emperor-beyond-the-Sea.

"You at least know the Magic which the Emperor put into

Narnia at the very beginning," she tells Aslan. "You know that every traitor belongs to me as my lawful prey and that for every treachery I have a right to a kill."[1] On these grounds, the White Witch demands Edmund's life. The law of the Deep Magic decrees that all evildoers will be given over to the powers of evil for destruction.

A similar "Deep Magic" is built into the foundations of our own world. "The wages of sin is death,"[2] the apostle Paul tells us. Sin is rebellion against God. It is rejecting his authority and acknowledging no other authority but the self. And we have all done just that. No exceptions. Paul tells us that "all have sinned and fall short of the glory of God."[3] We are all, like Edmund, traitors to God. As in Narnia, the law in our world is that all traitors shall be given over to the evil one for destruction.

When the White Witch invokes the Deep Magic and demands that Edmund be given to her to kill, the rational animals rise to defend the boy. But Aslan calms them. Yes, he concurs. What she says is true.

The children are horrified. Susan whispers in the Lion's ear:

> "Can't we do something about the Deep Magic? Isn't there something you can work against it?"
>
> "Work against the Emperor's magic?" said Aslan, turning to her with something like a frown on his face. And nobody ever made that suggestion to him again.[4]

In Narnia, as in our world, when a God ordains a law, that law has a deep and profound purpose and cannot be manipulated or countered. When Jesus gathers his closest friends and explains to them that he must go to Jerusalem and suffer terrible torture and death, Peter is determined to prevent it. He takes Jesus aside and says he is not about to let it happen. Jesus' rebuke is shockingly stern: "Get behind Me, Satan! You are an offense to Me, for you are not mindful of the things of God, but the things of men."[5] On earth, as in Narnia, the idea of bending the rules and plans of Deity gets no quarter from God.

ASLAN FINDS A WAY

Aslan will not flout the Deep Magic, but he will provide a solution to Edmund's deadly dilemma. He sends the assembly of creatures away and speaks alone with the White Witch. After the conference he announces that she has renounced her claim to Edmund's life. A great relief sweeps through the crowd. But as they make their camp for the night, the Lion becomes sad and withdrawn. Feeling that some terrible doom is hanging over Aslan, Susan and Lucy cannot sleep. They arise to look for him and find him walking slowly toward the wood, his head and tail hanging low. Aslan is glad of their company and wants them near him in his sadness.

The scene reminds us of the night before the crucifixion of Jesus, when he takes his three closest friends, Peter, James, and John, into the darkness of Gethsemane while he prays. "My soul is exceedingly sorrowful, even to death," he tells them. "Stay here and watch with Me."[6]

After a while Aslan must continue his walk toward the great Stone Table at the top of the mound. He forbids the children to follow him, but they watch from a distance and learn the reason for his sorrow and for Edmund's release. A hideous company awaits the Lion at the Stone Table—ogres, bull-headed men, spirits of evil trees and poisonous plants, hags, incubuses, wraiths, wolves, and other horrible creatures. And in the middle of them all stands the White Witch herself. At her command, the creatures bind, shave, and muzzle Aslan. He silently allows it, though one sweep of his paw would have been the death of them all. The creatures mock and jeer at the Lion as they kick him, hit him, and spit on him. He endures it without a word. With great effort they heave him onto the Stone Table where the White Witch prepares her deadly knife. Before delivering the blow, she gloats at Aslan:

And now, who has won? Fool, did you think that by all this you would save the human traitor? Now I will kill you instead of him as our pact was and so the Deep Magic will be appeased. But when you are dead what will prevent me from killing him as well? And who will take him out of my hand then? Understand that you have given me Narnia forever, you have lost your own life and you have not saved his. In that knowledge, despair and die.[7]

She raises her knife and kills the Lion.

Here the story echoes Jesus' silent acceptance of his fate. In spite of having at his immediate disposal battalions of angels to wipe his accusers and tormentors from the face of the earth, he refuses to call up this power. He chooses rather to suffer the mockery and torture of the soldiers and finally an agonizing death nailed to a Roman cross.

THE DEAL WITH THE DEVIL

The death of Aslan in Narnia illuminates the reasons for the death of Jesus. He takes the place of a condemned prisoner. He volunteers as a substitute for another who deserves to die and hasn't the power to escape the sentence. Edmund in Narnia is all of us. All humanity has betrayed God by rebelling against him and turning to ourselves. We are all condemned. He died in our place.

Although Edmund is one and we are many, the fact that Aslan dies for him alone points to an astounding truth. Jesus would have done the same for you had you been the only rebel in the universe. The parables of the lost sheep and the lost coin tell us that God's love for any one of us individually is so deep and intense that he will go to any length, including death, to get even one of us back.

The Narnian story goes one step further than the Gospels and gives us a clue as to what Satan may have been thinking when he crucified Christ. The gloat of the White Witch as she prepares to strike the blade into Aslan reveals the treachery of her heart. She made a deal with the Lion that she had no intention of keeping. Yes, she would gladly accept him as a substitute for Edmund and relinquish her claim on the boy. But with Aslan out of the way, there would be no power in Narnia to prevent her from taking Edmund as well, and all of Narnia too.

I have little doubt that this parallels the thinking of Satan. Yes, he will take Christ as a substitute and relinquish his claim on Adam and Eve and all their sin-tarnished descendants. But with Jesus out of the way, what's to hold him to that promise? He must have thought his attack on humanity had succeeded far beyond his wildest dreams. He had set out on a vengeful plot to turn God's pet creation project into chaos and ended up getting God himself in his clutches. With God destroyed, Satan's power would become unlimited. Nothing could stand in his way. He would destroy mankind, the earth, the universe, and then possibly the throne of God himself. In trying to make a deal with Satan, God had made a fatal miscalculation. Scruples are not a part of the devil's baggage.

Deeper Magic before the Dawn of Time

The death of Aslan devastates Lucy and Susan, who observe it from their hiding place. After the White Witch and her hideous army march off to defeat Peter and reclaim Narnia, the two girls approach the body of the Lion and stroke it tenderly, weeping until they have no more tears. They remove the horrid muzzle and try to untie the binding cords. The scene evokes a feeling reminiscent of the women coming to the tomb of Jesus the morning after the Crucifixion to prepare his body for burial.

As the sky lightens with the dawn, Susan and Lucy become chilled. They walk around to warm themselves. As their backs are turned away from the Stone Table and the body of the Lion, they hear a thunderous crack. They turn to see the Stone Table split in two, the Lion's body nowhere to be seen.

> "Oh, it's too bad," sobbed Lucy; "they might have left the body alone."
> "Who's done it?" cried Susan. "What does it mean? Is it more magic?"
> "Yes!" said a great voice behind their backs. "It is more magic." They looked round. There, shining in the sunrise, larger than they had seen him before, shaking his mane (for it had apparently grown again) stood Aslan himself.[8]

Aslan assures the girls that he is neither dead nor a ghost. They fling themselves upon him and cover him with kisses, reminding us of Jesus' invitation to the disciple Thomas to touch his wounds and know that he is indeed alive and solidly present in a real body.

Aslan is alive! The girls do not understand what has happened. He explains:

> Though the Witch knew the Deep Magic, there is a magic deeper still which she did not know. Her knowledge goes back only to the dawn of Time. But if she could have looked a little further back, into the stillness and the darkness before Time dawned, she would have read there a different incantation. She would have known that when a willing victim who had committed no treachery was killed in a traitor's stead, the Table would crack and Death itself would start working backward.[9]

This Deeper Magic from Before the Dawn of Time destroys the schemes of the White Witch without compromising the Deep Magic she invoked. She got her victim, just as the Deep Magic allowed. And she killed him, eliminating the only power in Narnia that could thwart her ambitions. But she did not know that she was taking a victim with the power to turn death on its heels and return to life.

Aslan's return to life breaks the Stone Table, meaning the old Deep Magic engraved upon it no longer works. Never again must traitors forfeit their lives into the White Witch's hands. The innocent victim has taken their place, and they can now choose to align with Aslan and be protected from the White Witch.

The Deeper Magic in Narnia echoes a reality in our own world. Before God made the universe and created man and woman, he was prepared for the possibility that they would turn traitor. He had a willing victim ready to step in just in case the humans rebelled. The apostle Peter tells us that Christ was "foreordained before the foundation of the world."[10] The "Deeper Magic" was in place, ready when needed. And when that need arose, Christ came to the rescue. He offered himself as the willing victim. But to Satan's consternation, he arose from the dead three days later, taking the weapon of death from the devil's hand. In thwarting the death due to rebels, Christ offers all victims a way out of death into his life.

Narnia's Stone Table breaks, signaling the end of the Deep Magic. It reminds us of the moment Christ died, when the massive curtain enclosing the holy place in the Jewish temple ripped apart from top to bottom. The holy place was called the holy of holies, where God resided. It was forbidden to all men and women except once a year on the Day of Atonement when the high priest entered on behalf of the people. The ripped curtain meant that God was no longer inaccessible. The sin that alienated us from God was taken care of. The power of the old law that said, "The soul who sins shall die" was destroyed and no longer threatened us. A substitute had been supplied.

Lewis was convinced that the sacrifice of Christ is a historical fact. He also believed that "the central Christian belief is that Christ's death has somehow put us right with God and given us a fresh start."[11] He knew that Christians hold varying ideas about just how Christ's death accomplished this, and that it can be expressed in many different ways. "You can say that Christ died for our sins. You may say that the Father has forgiven us because Christ has done for us what we ought to have done. You may say that we are washed in the blood of the Lamb. You may say that Christ has defeated death. They are all true."[12] His point is that these theories and expressions are less important than the fact of the Crucifixion itself. All of them may be helpful pictures, but none shows the enormity of the reality.

We don't know the deepest, multidimensional meanings behind the cosmic drama. But Lewis points out that we can accept a thing as true without knowing how it works. "A man can eat his dinner without knowing exactly how food nourishes him." Beneath all the theories and speculation, he identifies the foundational truth to which all Christians must hold: "We are told that Christ was killed for us, that His death has washed out our sins, and that by dying He disabled death itself. That is the formula. That is Christianity. That is what has to be believed."[13]

INCREDIBLE LOVE

In his sacrificial death for Edmund, Aslan shows the incredible love of the Lion for his Narnians. This sacrifice, which places the well-being of the beloved above the well-being of self, demonstrates the highest kind of love. The Greek word for this high, unselfish, sacrificial love is *agape*, which differs from other loves mentioned in the New Testament—affection *(storge)* and brotherly love *(phileo)*.

Jesus' love for us is agape. If you are like me, you find this love hard to fathom. Why would the Creator of the universe leave all the splendors of heaven and become one of his own creatures on this messed-up planet? Especially knowing he would be persecuted, misunderstood, hated, and finally tortured and killed? It's hard to wrap our minds around just how dearly he loves us. He created us for intimate companionship with him, and as incredible as it seems, he finds real delight in us. Before Adam and Eve fell, God met them every evening for a stroll through their beautiful Eden. And when the couple rejected him, he was heartbroken. He couldn't stand the thought of spending all eternity without us. We are more precious to him than heaven itself, so he came after us, determined to do whatever it took to get us back. The cost was Jesus' death on the cross, but that didn't matter. It was not too high a price if it would restore to him that intimate fellowship of God and man and woman that all enjoyed in Eden.

Although this love Jesus has for us is of the highest kind, it's not always easy for us to feel it. We express and receive love in two-way companionship, conversation, warmth, and affection shown in hugs and acts of tender care and kindness. Without the presence of Jesus in bodily form, we miss all that, and as a result his love may not seem as real as we would like. Of course the Gospels show abundant evidences not only of his sacrificial love but also of his loving care in his many healings and miracles to relieve suffering. And we have records of those incidents in which Jesus expressed tender affection and brotherly love, such as that touching lament over Jerusalem and his conversation with his disciples during the Last Supper. But the emphasis is (rightly) on the big idea—his enormous act of sacrifice by which he brought us back to him. The love is clear enough, but it may be easier to know it intellectually than to feel it emotionally.

Aslan helps us to feel God's love. He exudes warmth and affection, drawing us to connect with the Lion emotionally. He shows his love not only in the great sacrifice at the Stone Table but also in his obvious and oft-demonstrated affection for the children and creatures. Aslan romps and plays with Susan and Lucy. When Shasta falls on his feet before him, he kisses the boy on the forehead. He kisses the mare Hwin and calls her "dearest daughter." In *Prince Caspian* when Lucy first sees Aslan, she runs to him and buries her face in his mane as he embraces her. In the same story the talking beasts find Aslan irresistible and surge around him, fawning, rubbing, and touching. It's easy to love a God like this.

Aslan's warm love draws us to *feel* the truth about Christ that we find in the Gospels. Intellectual knowledge is wonderful, but without the feeling the love may seem only half real. The truth has greater impact when both the mind and the heart combine to turn knowledge into experience. This is Aslan's gift to us.

But can it be overdone? Can Aslan actually come between Jesus and us, leading us to love a fictional character instead of the real person? One concerned mother wrote to Lewis when her young son admitted that he loved Aslan more than he loved Jesus. Lewis replied:

> But Laurence can't *really* love Aslan more than Jesus, even if he feels that's what he is doing. For the things he loves Aslan for doing or saying are simply the things Jesus really did and said. So that when Laurence thinks he is loving Aslan, he is really loving Jesus: and perhaps loving him more than he ever did before.[14]

Aslan simply opened this boy's eyes and his heart to the truth about the love of God that he knew he should feel but had not felt as he read the Gospel accounts of Jesus. His nine-year-old heart responded to Aslan; in so doing, Laurence was really responding to all that Christ was and is—the deepest and most profound love that any mortal can know.

Aslan's love displaced the Deep Magic with Deeper Magic. That is simply an imaginative and vivid way of saying that Christ's love displaced the law of sin and death with the greater law of love that conquers death.

CHAPTER 7

ROMPING WITH THE LION

Fun, Happiness, and Joy

Aslan! Aslan! Have I made the first joke? Will everybody
always be told how I made the first joke?

—THE FIRST JACKDAW, *THE MAGICIAN'S NEPHEW*

After the White Witch executes Aslan, something happens that surprises not only Susan and Lucy but readers as well. The girls have remained with the body throughout the night, kissing the great Lion's face, stroking his beautiful fur, and crying until no tears are left. As dawn breaks, they walk about to shake off the nighttime chill.

Suddenly a thunderous boom shakes the earth. Startled, they turn and see that Aslan's body is gone. As the girls gape, they hear a voice behind them and turn to see Aslan himself, alive, real, healthy, and larger and more glorious than ever. That is surprise enough, but another quickly follows:

A mad chase began. Round and round the hilltop he led them, now hopelessly out of their reach, now letting them almost catch his tail, now diving between them, now tossing them in the air with his huge and beautifully velveted paws and catching them again, and now stopping unexpectedly so that all three of them rolled over together in a happy laughing heap of fur and arms and legs. It was such a romp as no one has ever had except in Narnia.[1]

After the tragedy of execution and the triumph of resurrection, the last thing we expect from the great Lion is wild cavorting in the morning grass. We expect him to display majesty, exultation, power, and perhaps joy, but surely a kind of noble, high-minded, and digni-fied joy—not a *romp*.

The New Testament describes nothing so wild as a chase or a game when the disciples meet the resurrected Jesus, but it does show them experiencing great joy. Jesus walked to Emmaus with two dis-ciples. He ate dinner with them and then disappeared, leaving them saying in wonder, "Did not our heart burn within us while He talked with us on the road, and while He opened the Scriptures to us?"[2] When he appeared to the eleven disciples in Jerusalem, both Luke and John tell us that they felt great joy and gladness in his presence.

If Lewis pushed expression of that joy beyond what the New Testament describes and made it into a romp, there is good reason. For one thing, the summary reports of the risen Jesus' appearances may not reflect the full intensity of what these people felt. Considering they were in the presence of someone they loved dearly who had just come back from the dead, it's likely that their elation could hardly be described. A hint of it appears in Peter when the disciples are fishing on Lake Galilee and see Jesus on the shore. The boat, dragging a full net of fish, moves too slowly for Peter. He can't wait; he jumps over-board and swims to Jesus.[3] With the Lion's delightful romp, Lewis, who is not reporting history but writing a story, conveys this extreme joy that people who love God would experience in his risen presence.

PLEASURE UNDER SUSPICION

I would guess that many devout Christians reading the *Chronicles* have no trouble with the God of Narnia rolling in the grass and playing tag, but they would be quite uncomfortable with the idea of Jesus doing it. They may easily accept the many expressions of joy, humor, feasting, dancing, and partying that fill these books because they are fantasy, but they would shy away from much of it in real life. Although Christians believe in joy, many of us have trouble abandoning ourselves to it. We can get so serious about living a disciplined Christian life that we become wary of frivolity.

Some Christians even subject themselves to deliberate severity and discomfort. We see the extremes of this in the historical acts of penance required of sinners—the practice of self-flagellation for no other purpose than to experience the pain of Jesus or stifle frivolous thoughts, the prohibiting of spontaneous singing in monasteries, and the puritanical repression of innocent pleasures.

We are only a generation past the days when Christians were characterized mainly by what they did not do. Though the restrictions varied from one denomination to another, the list of don'ts was extensive: Christians did not dance, drink, smoke, attend plays or movies, permit mixed swimming, gamble, wear shorts, play card games, wear makeup, celebrate Christmas, or play musical instruments. Of course at least one item on this list—smoking—is definitely harmful. Others, such as drinking, have a potential for harm that many feel outweighs any possible benefit. My purpose here is not to evaluate the relative acceptability of these prohibitions but to show that Christians at one time or another have found virtually all pleasures suspect.

Although few Christians hold to these prohibitions today, the attitude that bred them lingers. And the reason is simple: Pleasure can lead to sin. Drinking a glass of wine now and then may be all right in and of itself, but one thing can lead to another, and the next thing you know it's a second glass, then a bottle, and then you are an alcoholic. A ballroom dance with your husband or wife may be perfectly innocent, but if you dance, so will your teens, holding each other close while raging hormones spawn temptations hard to resist. Considering the human tendency toward excess, Christians often insist on the course of safety and ban the pleasure to prevent its abuse.

Christians have found at least one other reason to restrain joy and pleasure. In the Middle Ages it was thought that too much pleasure was an affront to the gravity of the sacrifice Christ made for us. Many Christians then and since have emulated the Christ who carried upon himself the sins and sorrows of the world. They kept before them at all times the image of Christ's sufferings and God's disappointment with us for our failure to follow his will. Joy, fun, feasting, and happiness simply did not enter the picture.

That attitude has lingered in subsequent generations and remains with many Christians even today. It explains why Christians have been accused of going about with long faces and putting a damper on fun. Yes, they know the apostle Paul said to "rejoice in the Lord always,"[4] but he must have meant a restrained, internalized feeling of rightness that comes from resisting temptation and keeping one's self untainted by the world. Surely he didn't mean we should really enjoy life as non-Christians do.

PARTY ANIMALS

In both Narnia and the Bible we get an altogether different picture. Christians should enjoy life *more* than non-Christians do. In *The Magician's Nephew* Lewis asserts that joy should prevail in spite of the enormity of God's sacrifice. Shortly after creation Aslan addresses the evil that has come into his world in the form of Jadis the witch. "Evil will come of that evil," he says, "but it is still a long way off, and I will see to it that the worst falls upon myself. In the meantime, let us take such order that for many hundred years yet this shall be a merry land in a merry world."[5] As we read the rest of the stories, we see that Narnia is indeed a merry land of joy, feasting, dancing, jesting, and laughter.

Is it ever!

It starts on the very day of creation when the newly created jackdaw inadvertently makes—or rather becomes—the first joke. The animals try to suppress their laughter, but Aslan tells them to let it out: "Laugh and fear not, creatures. Now that you are no longer dumb and witless, you need not always be grave. For jokes as well as justice come in with speech."[6]

Narnia is a place of joy, laughter, celebration, feasting, and humor. All inhibitions are loosed, and the creatures revel in the good that Aslan provides. Toward the end of *The Lion, the Witch and the Wardrobe*, Peter, Susan, Edmund, and Lucy are crowned kings and queens of Narnia, "and that night there was a great feast in Cair Paravel, and revelry and dancing, and gold flashed and wine flowed."[7] In *The Silver Chair* Jill looks out of the tunnel from the Underland and sees fauns and dryads dancing to wild, intensely sweet music, and she knows she is in Narnia.[8] In *The Horse and His Boy* a great feast is held on the lawn of the castle at Anvard after the defeat of Rabadash the Calormene. "And the wine flowed and tales were told and jokes were cracked," after which a poet, fiddlers, and storytellers filled the night with tales and songs.[9]

The wildest of all Narnian celebrations occurs in *Prince Caspian*, when the creatures gather about Aslan and march against Miraz and the Telmarines. The tree spirits, birch-girls, willow-women, queenly beeches, shaggy oak-men, and others bow and curtsy and wave their long, thin arms toward the Lion. They dance around him, and soon others enter the dance and caper among the swaying trees, including a youth dressed only in a fawn-skin (who turns out to be Bacchus, the god of wine) with a company of girls just as wild. "There's a chap who might do anything—absolutely anything," Edmund tells Lucy. Silenus enters on a donkey, and the dance accelerates to a frenzy. Vines sprout and weave in and out of the dance, throwing about grapes with a taste sweet beyond imagination. What mouths the grapes don't fill ring with laughter and shouting and yodeling. Aslan stands in the midst of it all, thoroughly approving. The reveling continues until all collapse from happy exhaustion as the sun rises. Edmund turns to Lucy and says, "I wouldn't have felt safe with Bacchus and all his wild girls if we'd met them without Aslan." And Lucy replies, "I should think not."[10]

If Aslan's romp makes us uptight Christians uncomfortable, what does this all-night party do? Our Christian heritage and fear of our human weaknesses have led us to put such partying on the side of the devil instead of God. You've heard comedians say they would rather go to hell than heaven, because that's where all the fun is. Stereotypically Christianity has nothing to do with "wine, women, and song," so in the popular imagination those things are the property of hell. And Christians concede all too easily, forgetting that God created everything, and all was meant for joy. The wild revel in *Prince Caspian* reminds us that these joys belong not to the evil one but to the people of God. The devil has nothing of his own. All he can do is lure us into misusing the good God gives. The all-important key is in what Edmund says to Lucy: "I wouldn't have felt safe with Bacchus and all his wild girls if we'd met them without Aslan." The presence of God makes all the difference.

Lewis affirms this principle for adults in his novel *That Hideous Strength*. Fleeing from a great evil, the thoroughly modern young heroine Jane Studdock finds refuge with a small band of Christians at a country manor. Her estranged husband is about to return. After Jane prepares their bedchamber, a wildly beautiful woman enters, dressed in a flame-colored robe that exposes her large breasts. Gnomelike little men in red caps dance and somersault about the room, making shambles of the bed clothing, as ivy, honeysuckle, and red roses proliferate everywhere.

The head of the little Christian company explains to Jane that her vision affirmed the flaming pleasure of joyful sexuality. She is shocked. All her preconceptions are turned upside down. "It ought to have been she who was saying these things to the Christians. Hers ought to have been the vivid, perilous world brought against their grey formalized one; hers the quick, vital movements and theirs the stained glass attitudes."[11]

Jane has bought into a lie. It's really the Christians who have all the good stuff. The other side has stolen it, peeled it raw, put it on tawdry display, and offers it cheap but without warranty. Edmund is right: God's presence makes the difference.

JOY IN THE BIBLE

In presenting joy, fun, humor, and celebration as the characteristics of God's creatures, Lewis reflects what we find in the Bible. Notice the unrestrained joy in this psalm:

> Praise Him with the sound of the trumpet;
> Praise Him with the lute and harp!
> Praise Him with the timbrel and dance;
> Praise Him with stringed instruments and flutes!
> Praise Him with loud cymbals;
> Praise Him with clashing cymbals![12]

These musicians are really getting into it, dancing as they blow and strum and bang on their instruments. Praising God with loud cymbals is not enough: "Praise Him with clashing cymbals!" the psalmist urges. Don't hold back. Make those pan lids ring!

King David was so joyful over the return of the ark of the covenant to Israel that he leapt and whirled at the head of the parade that brought it into Jerusalem, shocking the sensibilities of his wife Michal.[13]

Jesus did not meet the rigid and joyless expectations of the religious establishment with all its stifling legal restrictions. As a result he was labeled a glutton and a wino. His first miracle was to make a hundred gallons of the finest wine for a wedding celebration—alcoholic beverage for a party! He told his critics they shouldn't expect his disciples to be austere while he was around. "Can the friends of the bridegroom fast while the bridegroom is with them?"[14] His presence is a cause for celebration.

And the Bible is not without humor. If we could read it without a religious filter (that watchful dragon), we might recognize many comic moments. When Jesus spoke of a camel squeezing through the eye of a needle, or of straining out a gnat but swallowing a camel, or of a log hanging from the eye of a man trying to pick a speck of dust from the eye of another, his audiences must have brayed in laughter. Sometimes the humor in the Bible is merely a wry comment, like that of the Philistine king of Gath when told that David, escaping Saul and feigning madness, wanted to join him. His reply was a dig at his courtiers, "Have I need of madmen?"[15] (Translation: Don't I have enough crazy people around me already?) And then there's Elijah's taunt to the priests of Baal when their prayers to their god failed to ignite the altar on Mount Carmel: "You'll have to shout louder. . . . Perhaps he is deep in thought, or he is relieving himself. Or maybe he is away on a trip, or he is asleep and needs to be wakened!"[16] Humor is not off-limits to God's people. It is part of our most sacred writings, and some of it came from the lips of Jesus himself.

Readers may find it interesting that C. S. Lewis himself hardly fit the mold of the long-faced Christian. He was not the shy, hesitant, soft-spoken introvert portrayed by Anthony Hopkins in the 1994 movie Shadowlands but rather a big, gregarious, sometimes boisterous man with a booming voice and a loud laugh. He liked nothing better than an evening with his friends at a favorite Oxford pub, quaffing ale, telling stories, cracking jokes, and making puns. He also smoked, though when he learned of its hazards he tried to quit. But no one who knew him or even met him briefly doubted the reality of his Christian commitment. Ultraconservative American fundamentalist evangelist Bob Jones met Lewis in Oxford in 1953. Afterward he told biographer Walter Hooper, "That man smokes a pipe, and that man drinks liquor—but I *do* believe he is a

Christian!"[17] Hooper later called Lewis "the most thoroughly *converted* man I ever met."[18]

QUARANTINING PLEASURE

Christians can rightfully enjoy any pleasure God gives them, but they do encounter two legitimate reasons for deliberately shunning it. In the Sermon on the Mount, Jesus said, "If your right eye causes you to sin, pluck it out and cast it from you; for it is more profitable for you that one of your members perish, than for your whole body to be cast into hell."[19] Each of us finds certain temptations hard to resist. A perfectly innocent pleasure that for you may be no temptation at all may be so irresistible to me that I cannot enjoy it in moderation, but will indulge to harmful excess. I must exercise discipline and cut myself off from that particular pleasure. It may be good for others, but it is fatal to me.

What I must not do, however, is impose my ban on you. The very thing that would bring my downfall may be to you a joy that opens the portals of heaven and reveals the character of God. I must not insist that my weakness deny you that joy. Just because I must make myself "one-eyed" does not give me the right to blind others.

Years ago I read a book by a prominent Christian who condemned Michelangelo's statue of David for its nudity. At about the same time I heard a radio message by a respected evangelist who had just seen the statue in Italy and effusively praised its beauty. I wrote asking him how to resolve the contradiction. The thoughtful answer from his assistant emphasized the words of the apostle Paul: "Everything is pure to those whose hearts are pure. But nothing is pure to those who are corrupt and unbelieving, because their minds and consciences are defiled."[20]

At first this answer didn't satisfy me. "It's all right as long as your mind is pure" could rationalize absolutely any indulgence. But in time I realized that a pure and undefiled mind is that polarized lens that filters out the evil of the Fall and reveals the good in creation. A pure mind sees the glory in beauty without the contamination of lust. But there are dangers. No mind is pure enough to filter out everything that can tempt, so there are obvious limits as to how close to the edge we should get. We can easily deceive ourselves and hide lust under a pretense of pure appreciation. That danger, however, is always present in all good, and we cannot demand a course of safety that denies to all any good that can tempt a few. I must not quarantine a pleasure for everyone just because I lack resistance to it myself. Living a joyful life reflects the character of Aslan—not safe, but good.

DENYING HAPPINESS FOR THE SAKE OF OTHERS

Here is the other reason why Christians must sometimes choose pain over pleasure. We are told to rejoice with those who rejoice but also weep with those who weep. Christians are to "bear one another's burdens."[21] Lewis notes that great sacrifices of happiness "may be necessary that it may be more widely distributed. All may have to be a little hungry in order that none may starve. But do not let us mistake necessary evils for good."[22] The purpose of bearing pain is not for its own sake or because there is any inherent virtue in the experience of it, but because our love for others wants their pain relieved. Jesus did not want to bear the pain of the cross; he prayed fervently that it would be removed from him. Yet because it was necessary for our well-being, he bore it willingly. Lewis wrote to an American child that sometimes one must give up fun in order to do good, but that "giving up fun for no other reason except that you think it's 'good' to give it up is all nonsense."[23]

Aslan submitted to pain so that joy could be increased in Narnia. This illustrates Lewis's conviction that "joy is the serious business of Heaven."[24] Down here in the Shadowlands, we indulge in frivolity only in our moments of leisure. But in heaven joy will be our full-time occupation. Joy is what God is about, and it's what we must be about too. We were created for joy. All creation shows it. Christ died so that we could escape the misery our enemy inflicted and live the joy he intended. To live in needless gloom is to reject a gift for which he paid a great price. We find our joy in being restored to Christ, and it is available in no other way. Each time we experience the delights of creation, our minds should travel up the beam to him as the Source, and we should shout our thankfulness and express it by being as joyful as he meant us to be.

JOY: THE REAL THING

We've said much about pleasure, happiness, fun, and joy, as if they were synonymous. But now it's time to separate the reality from its shadow. Joy is a thing apart, and it is to happiness as a well is to a cup of water. We've discussed how Christians can be joyful even when experiencing pain or deep difficulties. Happiness is an emotion of the moment, an emotion caused by external circumstances—a winning lottery ticket, a luxurious bath at the end of a hard day, a new job, a good movie, a day at the beach, a steak at your favorite restaurant. But joy does not depend on pleasure or good things happening. It is a solid, permanent, secure foundation that underlies your life and withstands all that can be thrown against you. You can miss out on the satisfactions and pleasures listed above and still have that underlying joy.

In *The Silver Chair*, when the Underland earthmen capture Puddleglum and the two children, Jill Pole despairs, wondering what will become of them. "Now don't you let your spirits down, Pole," says the marsh-wiggle. "There's one thing you've got to remember. We're back on the right lines. We were to go under the Ruined City, and we *are* under it. We're following the instructions again."[25]

Puddleglum is known as a pessimist, but here his spirits are high. He is joyful. Obviously his good feelings do not result from delightful circumstances. Puddleglum is not happy to be captured by enemies, nor does he find pleasure in that dreary, evil underworld. He is joyful because he knows he is in the will of Aslan, and that is exactly where he wants to be. His joy is not dependent on the circumstance but on the Lion.

Doing the hard thing even at the expense of comfort and immediate happiness does not make the Christian life one of perpetual misery. In following God through difficulty, we find real joy instead of its superficial substitute, happiness.

The apostle Paul, who wrote so much about joy, often wrote of it from prison cells. His life was anything but easy. He was stoned, shipwrecked, beaten, and imprisoned. When he was flogged and thrown into prison with his companion, Silas, the two men could not help but burst into song. You can have joy in the middle of devastating losses. That joy comes from knowing you are in the hands of a loving God who wills your ultimate good whatever the circumstance of the moment.

In *Prince Caspian* Aslan leads a march toward the camp of the Telmarines. A joyous company of followers collects around him. As they come to Beruna, bringing great merriment and joy, only a few in the town catch the spirit and join the revelers. Most hunker down and remain in their stunted, prosaic lives. Why do people reject joy? Most of them simply cannot understand what it's really like, because they have never experienced it. And there is no way to experience it until you join the march. You cannot know joy until you take a leap of faith and plunge into God's hands like a child into a swimming pool.

PART 2

LIVING LIKE A NARNIAN

CHAPTER 8

SLAYING THE DRAGON INSIDE

Kicking the Sin Habit

That dragon face in the pool was his own reflection.
There was no doubt of it. . . .
He had turned into a dragon while he was asleep.

—THE VOYAGE OF THE DAWN TREADER

———◦•◦•◦———

There was a boy called Eustace Clarence Scrubb, and he almost deserved it,"[1] begins *The Voyage of the Dawn Treader*. Lucy and Edmund are forced to spend a few weeks with this pill of a cousin while their parents are away on a business trip. Eustace has been brought up on the latest theories about discipline and education, and he thinks his tastes and insights are superior to everyone else's. Bullying and argumentative, he makes life miserable for his two guests.

One afternoon Edmund and Lucy manage a moment away from Eustace. As they gaze with pleasure at a picture of an archaic sailing ship on the wall, Eustace enters and ridicules the painting, starting an argument. Suddenly the waves in the picture move, and the three children are magically pulled toward the expanding frame of the painting. The next moment they are swimming in the sea, and soon afterward the crew of the ship pulls them on board.

The ship turns out to be a Narnian vessel, the *Dawn Treader*, which is carrying the young Prince Caspian on a quest. Caspian does all he can to make the three children comfortable, but Eustace finds fault with everything. He blames everyone for his being there and complains of his quarters, his food, and his treatment. As the voyage continues, he tries to bully the only passenger smaller than he is, the talking mouse Reepicheep. When water becomes scarce, he even tries to steal more than his ration.

The ship lands for repairs on a deserted, mountainous island, and Eustace slips away to avoid work. As he wanders among the mountain crags, a heavy fog rolls in and he gets lost. To his horror, he happens upon a huge dragon and hides in terror. But the dragon is sick and dies as Eustace watches. He finds shelter in the dragon's cave and falls asleep.

When Eustace awakens, he looks in a pool and finds, to his horror, the face of a dragon looking back at him. "Sleeping on a dragon's hoard with greedy, dragonish thoughts in his heart, he had become a dragon himself."[2] As the unthinkable fact sinks in, his first thought is that he can now get even with everyone. To his surprise, he doesn't want to. As a dragon he is cut off from the human race, and for the first time in his life, he longs for companionship. Thoughts he has never considered invade his mind, and he wonders if he has been as good as he has always thought himself to be. Finding that he now has the tastes of a dragon, he eats the dead dragon for breakfast. The gruesome act makes him hate what he has become. He is almost afraid to be alone with himself, but he is ashamed to be with his companions.

Eustace's conscience has awakened, and he realizes he has been a terrible nuisance. He finally returns to the camp and makes himself known to his companions. He now does his best to help the others, using his dragon strength to deliver a tree for the ship's new mast and his dragon breath to start cooking fires. But he is still a dragon, and knowing it makes him miserable.

EXPOSING THE DRAGON

Eustace is contending with a problem that hides in the heart of every human born since Adam and Eve. When forced to look at the truth about ourselves, as Eustace did in the pool, we realize that we are, at heart, dragons, ugly and hideous, with virtually every thought directed only toward our selves—our needs, our wants, our images. The word that sums it up is *pride*. Pride was the original sin of Adam and Eve, and pride is the embedded sin that ruins our inner nature and turns us into dragons.

What? Me a dragon? you may think. *Sure, I'm not perfect. I have a few little flaws and commit a little sin now and then, but who doesn't? I'm not a thief or a murderer and not even a brat like Eustace. Really, to think of myself as a dragon is a little over the top, don't you think?* I know we all think that way, but before we dismiss the dragon label as overstatement, let's look a little deeper.

As we explained in chapter 4, God designed us to be bearers of his image. God wanted one being in his world that would reflect his own nature. He wanted one creature that would show to the rest of creation the exact nature of God himself. To bear the image of God was the glory and purpose of the newly created Adam and Eve. As long as they remained within the will of God, he remained in intimate fellowship with them, and thus they fulfilled their purpose, which made them continually and ecstatically happy.

God intended to be the guiding light in our lives, leading us always into joy. But Satan convinced the first man and woman that they didn't need God—that they had what it took to run their own lives. Pride in their own strength took over, and they rebelled against God and kicked him out. It was like a man who has never flown a plane firing the pilot of his corporate jet in midair and sitting down at the controls himself. He is doomed to crash because he is not equal to the task. He has no idea how to run the machine.

Adam and Eve in their fallen condition did not know how to run the human machine, and they passed on that condition to all their descendants. Ever since they rejected God, pride has dominated the human race. The philosophy of man has been "I can do it myself." We have fooled ourselves into believing we can find within ourselves the inner strength to make the world a better place and control our own destiny. It has never worked, it isn't working now, and it will never work. The history of the world displays the disaster of self without God. Wars, slavery, cruelty, oppression, poverty, exploitation, and tyranny have always been the lot of humanity, and it continues even now. Ours is a history of self looking out for self—of selves trampling other selves to assert their own superiority.

Pride is the spring from which all other sins flow. The idea that self is king generates all of mankind's evils. Greed is simply the craving of more and more for self. Envy and covetousness are the desiring of what another has that self does not have. Lust and gluttony seek pleasure for the self. Lying deflects a problem, prevents discomfort, achieves an end, or shifts the blame for the benefit of self. All the attention is on the self. The total focus on self that makes dragons of us all is embedded in our nature.

If we think we're pretty good because we don't murder or steal and live generally decent lives, it's because we've lost the vision of what we were created to be. If mankind had not fallen, there would be no sin at all—not even little white lies. Absolutely perfect behavior would be simply normal for everyone, all the time. It would be nothing more than what God intended from the beginning. Refusing to recognize our dragon nature is dangerous. It's a kind of pride that ignores the truth and hides behind supposed superiorities.

No Little Sins

I would never claim that some sins are not worse than others. Mass murder is obviously worse than rolling past a stop sign on an isolated country road. But there is this about any sin at all, even that tiny insignificant private habit you think little about: It reveals a deeper problem inside.

In *The Horse and His Boy* the talking warhorse Bree is concerned about looking undignified when he rolls in the grass. Surely we can find nothing sinful about that; it's even a little funny. But as we read on, we see other things about Bree that tell us this little concern about his image may be the tip of an iceberg indicating a much more deadly problem in the horse's soul. Indeed we soon realize that Bree is a prideful horse who is highly impressed with himself. For example, when he and the mare Hwin reach a river, he turns aside, saying it's too wide for her to swim. But he actually thinks it's too wide for him as well. He expresses disdain for horses that only draw chariots in battles, seeing them as something less than real warhorses like himself. He bristles at the suggestion that he could be disguised as a mere packhorse to get the little company of four refugees safely through Calormen. He makes excuses to delay entering Narnia because he doesn't want to arrive there until his clipped tail grows out again.

Bree's pride shows in his preoccupation with his own supposed superiority. The self is at the control center of his being. It's all fully revealed when a sudden danger threatens and Bree's self-protective impulse automatically kicks in, driving him to flee at full speed, leaving his friends to fend for themselves. The experience undoes the great warhorse because he learns the truth about what he is inside. Bree is shamed for his cowardice and failure to meet the expectations he has set for himself. For a long time he thinks he has lost everything. The wise hermit of the Southern March, however, tells him that he has lost only his self-conceit. Of course he was braver and nobler than the dumb horses in Calormen, but he will be nothing special in Narnia. "As long as you know you're nobody very special," the hermit says, "you'll be a very decent sort of Horse."[3]

Toward the end of Bree's story, we see what may account for his foolish pride. For a long time he has lived away from Narnia and has a poor understanding of the true nature of the Lion. He thinks all the language about Aslan being a real lion is metaphorical. He believes in an absent, spiritualized deity that acted in the distant past—not a near and present reality that can change lives. With such a sterile theology, it's hardly surprising that he would center his life on himself. As Bree is explaining these beliefs to the Calormene girl Aravis, the Lion himself appears. And just as the resurrected Jesus dispelled the doubts of his disciple Thomas, Aslan invites Bree to touch him and know that he is a real beast. Thoroughly abashed but finally facing reality, Bree admits to being a fool. "Happy the Horse who knows that while he is still young. Or the Human either,"[4] says Aslan.

Although Lewis does not use the image of a dragon in Bree's story, the horse had inside him the same dragon as Eustace Scrubb—the dragon of pride, which Christians call the sin nature. In Bree it takes a somewhat different form than in the boy. Eustace is utterly driven by the dragon with no moderating influences. He has never been a Christian and has no concept of conformity to any principle of rightness. Bree, on the other hand, is a Narnian. And though he has long been away from the kingdom, he knows what good is and wants to conform to it. But being a powerful and magnificent warhorse, he thinks he can do it by his own strength. Eustace never even thinks about good and evil until that morning he realizes he is a dragon, and then he wants to change. But neither Eustace nor Bree has the power to do it.

Clawing at the Scales

One night the Lion approaches the dragon Eustace and bids him follow him to a mountain garden and pool. Aslan tells him to undress. Eustace scratches and scrapes off his dragon skin only to discover another inside it. He proceeds to scrape and claw himself out of that skin as well, but the skin beneath it is still a dragon's. After three attempts, all with the same result, Eustace is still a dragon.

The prevalent idea is that if we act like dragons, we can change. We can improve ourselves—focus on higher ideals, learn to respect one another, live more selflessly, and transform the planet with peace and love. Many think the reason Jesus came was to teach us a better way to live. If we will but heed his words and follow his example, we will improve our lives to where we qualify for heaven. This is far from the truth.

We can't change ourselves any more than Eustace could. We can strip away a sin as he stripped away a skin, but no matter how deep we go, we encounter more sins. Getting rid of bothersome sins does not change the inner fallen self. No matter how many skins we strip away, the horrid truth about what we are remains: We are dragons through and through, and we can't help but act accordingly. Just as Eustace couldn't help doing dragonish things, such as eating other dragons and raw meat, we commit evil in spite of our best resolve. Though we may improve the way we act externally, little thoughts betray us. We may sit up with a sick friend, mow a widow's lawn, help a stranded motorist, teach Sunday school, give a fortune to the church, and spend Saturdays feeding the homeless, all the while hoping in our hearts that people will notice and do us honor. We may by sheer will power conquer a sin or make an improvement, but, as Bree discovered, it takes but a crisis to expose the real truth. You may think you've conquered your temper until a rude driver cuts you off in traffic. As Lewis wryly notes in *The Screwtape Letters*, even the moment we think we've achieved humility, we become proud of it.

The plight of the alcoholic or addict typifies the truth inside every one of us. We are addicted to sin. Our race tasted the fruit, and now we all crave it, as Edmund craved Turkish delight. And we can't resist it. We are dragons, and we cannot get rid of our dragon cravings.

As Eustace discovers, shedding skin after skin doesn't do any good. No matter how many skins he strips away, he is still a dragon. He needs a complete change at the core, and he can't make it happen. Left on his own, he is doomed to be a dragon until he dies. Without God we're like burned-out light bulbs. No amount of shining up and polishing will make us light up. We can't be improved or repaired; we must be changed.

Shedding the Scales

After Eustace fails repeatedly to get rid of his dragon skin, Aslan says to him, "You will have to let me undress you." Though Eustace fears the Lion's claws, he is desperate, so he rolls over on his back and allows him to do his work. The Lion cuts deep, and it hurts Eustace terribly. But it feels good to have the dragon skin come away. Then Aslan throws him into the pool. The water burns painfully at first, but soon it feels wonderful. Shortly afterward, the Lion takes him out and dresses him in all new clothes.

Thus Eustace is changed from being a dragon in the only way possible. He could not do it on his own. Only the Lion could strip away the hideous skin and scales and restore him to the boy whom Aslan intended all along.

The whole idea behind the Christian religion is restoration of the creation ideal. (In fact, the root meaning of the word *religion* is to reconnect—to re-ligature or re-ligament.) God wants to restore to every human the close and loving relationship that he had with Adam and Eve before they fell. He wants to replace that self-seeking sin nature with his own nature. He wants to replace our dragon hearts with himself. But he will not act against our wills. Our freedom is so vital to our humanity that God will not violate it, even in our best interests. He will not kill the dragon inside and give us his Holy Spirit unless we desire it. Just as Eustace gave up trying to change himself and allowed Aslan to do it for him, we, too, must volunteer for the operation.

Aslan throwing Eustace into the pool is a picture of Christian baptism. When we allow God to kill our dragon selves, we undergo a kind of death, indicated by the baptismal burial in water. The new undragoned life we receive in the Holy Spirit is something like a resurrection, which is pictured by coming out of the water. Baptism is also a kind of washing, getting rid of the filth of sin and coming out clean and pure. The new clothing Aslan then gives Eustace pictures God giving us a new nature, dressing us freely in the goodness we cannot achieve. Consider the words of the prophet Isaiah:

> My soul shall be joyful in my God;
> For He has clothed me with the garments of salvation,
> He has covered me with the robe of righteousness.[5]

Winning the Battle Inside

Ending his account of this episode in Eustace's life, Lewis tells us that "it would be nice, and fairly nearly true, to say that 'from that time forth Eustace was a different boy.' To be strictly accurate, he began to be a different boy. He had relapses. . . . But most of those I shall not notice. The cure had begun."[6]

These lapses in good behavior bring up a question that often confuses people about the Christian life. Why didn't Eustace's behavior change immediately and completely? When Jesus kills the old dragon, our sin nature, and fills us with his Holy Spirit, why don't we stop sinning? It's a little cumbersome to explain, but bear with me.

When we talk of killing the old nature, we are speaking metaphorically. But the metaphor expresses a real truth. It means that once you have the Holy Spirit in your life, he defeats the old nature and it no longer has power over you. You might say that the old nature has been mortally wounded, but its death throes still give you grief. You must choose whether to revive the slain dragon or draw on the power of the Holy Spirit to push it back into its coffin.

Some days you do better than others. Your life with the Spirit will never be perfect; no one can follow him perfectly. But his presence in you gives you the strength to hold to the right that you did not have before. The apostle Paul experienced the same conflict and described it this way:

> I know I am rotten through and through so far as my old sinful nature is concerned. No matter which way I turn, I can't make myself do right. I want to, but I can't. When I want to do good, I don't. And when I try not to do wrong, I do it anyway. But if I am doing what I don't want to do, I am not really the one doing it; the sin within me is doing it.
>
> It seems to be a fact of life that when I want to do what is right, I inevitably do what is wrong. I love God's law with all my heart. But there is another law at work within me that is at war with my mind.[7]

If the apostle Paul fought this battle between the dragon self and the new nature, why should we be surprised that we also fight it?

But there's good news. When we invite God into our lives, he doesn't hold these lapses against us. He understands what it's like to fight dragons; he's been there, done that, and won the battle for you. As Paul says further, "So now there is no condemnation for those who belong to Christ Jesus. For the power of the life-giving Spirit has freed you through Christ Jesus from the power of sin that leads to death."[8] The dragon can harass you, but it cannot reclaim you. Its power over you has been killed. That's what it means to call the sin nature dead. In weak moments you may revert to your old dragonish nature, but as long as you hate those moments and truly maintain your intention to live by the Spirit, God stays with you and counts your intentions as the real thing.

When my daughters were in grade-school band, I loved their concerts. A neighbor asked me why. How could I stand all the missed beats and sour notes? I told him, "Well, I guess I just hear what they intend." God hears what we intend. He loves hearing us attempt to play his music, sour notes and all. As long as we choose to play it, he keeps us dressed in those clean new uniforms—those robes of righteousness—to identify us as members of his band.

The new Eustace is not perfect, but he *begins* to be a better boy. In actuality he is a new person; he is no longer a dragon. His behavior will catch up as he conforms more each day to the Spirit of the Lion.

The Fine Paradox

If we don't kill the dragon of pride, it will stand between us and all possibility of joy. When the Lion's army defeats the Telmarines in *Prince Caspian*, Aslan gives the usurpers the choice of remaining in Narnia under King Caspian or being sent to a land in another dimension. The Telmarine leaders don't want to live in a country where they cannot rule the roost, so they choose the other world. Their choice reminds us of the terrible pride of Milton's Satan, who says, "'Tis better to rule in hell than to serve in heaven." *If I can't be at the top of the heap, I'm outta here. I would rather be alone and in charge of self than to be happy.*

In Caspian we find the opposite attitude. After the Telmarines are defeated, Aslan asks the prince if he feels ready to be king of Narnia.

> "I—I don't think I do, Sir," said Caspian. "I'm only a kid."
>
> "Good," said Aslan. "If you had felt yourself sufficient, it would have been a proof that you were not. Therefore, under us and under the High King, you shall be King of Narnia, Lord of Cair Paravel, and Emperor of the Lone Islands."[9]

Here we see the fine paradox that is affirmed over and over in Scripture: It's the humble who will be exalted. Wedding customs in biblical Judea required that guests be seated according to the honor they were due. Jesus said that someone attending a wedding should never seat himself in the highest place. The guest risks being shamed when the host asks him to move to a lower position. Rather, Jesus advised sitting in the lowest seat, "so that when he who invited you comes he may say to you, 'Friend, go up higher.' Then you will have glory in the presence of those who sit at the table with you. For whoever exalts himself will be humbled, and he who humbles himself will be exalted."[10]

The exalting that God has in store for us is something far above mere seating at a wedding feast. He holds out a promise even more extravagant than that of Aslan to Prince Caspian. The apostles Paul and John both tell us that we shall reign with him.[11] Reign over what? I can hardly imagine. But it's a stunning thought. The offer is on the table for us simple, bumbling, created humans to be coregents with the Lord of the universe, maybe over yet-to-be-populated planets, solar systems, or galaxies. Incredible? Not necessarily. Perhaps this explains the unending vastness and emptiness of deep space. Its emptiness is not barrenness but potential. It is waiting to be filled. And it's got to be big enough for God's creativity and love to expand forever. Whatever he has in mind, we fit somewhere into the plan. He intends for us to participate in whatever he has in store for all eternity.

There you have it. That is his promise to all who let him kill the dragon of pride and humbly submit to hosting the Holy Spirit in their lives. We've got some kind of future ahead of us.

CHAPTER 9

FOLLOW THE SIGNS
Knowing God's Will and Doing It

Aslan's instructions always work: there are no exceptions.
— PUDDLEGLUM, THE SILVER CHAIR

In *The Silver Chair* Aslan sends Eustace Scrubb and his classmate Jill Pole on a mission of huge importance to Narnia. Little do the children realize that one of their most difficult tasks will be to figure out how to follow the Lion's instructions. You'd think that when God speaks—in Narnia or in our world—knowing how to follow would be absolutely clear. But things seldom work out so easily.

When the story begins, Eustace and Jill are running as if their lives depend on it. Eustace, now back in England and a much better boy after having been a dragon, is helping Jill escape from school bullies. Both know all too well what will happen if they are caught. They scramble up the slope of the schoolyard, ducking under the laurels and weaving their way through the shrubbery. They hear their tormentors close behind as they approach the high wall that encloses the school. They have little hope of escape; the door is seldom open.

"'It's sure to be no good,' said Eustace with his hand on the handle; and then, 'O-o-oh. By Gum!!' For the handle turned and the door opened."[1]

But instead of the gray, heathery slope of the dismal moor outside the wall, the children see a clear blue sky and smooth, rich turf

95

bathed in bright sunlight. The bullies disappear. In awe Eustace and Jill walk through a lonely forest of majestic trees until they reach a cliff so high that they look down upon clouds far below. Eustace draws back, but Jill, showing off, stands at the dangerous edge. The height dizzies her, and she begins to faint and fall.

In his attempt to save her, Eustace falls over the cliff.

Jill comes to her senses and is horrified. She sees a brightly colored animal rush to the cliff. Blowing from his wide-opened mouth, he floats the falling boy safely across the sky until he disappears on the horizon.

I've already related Jill's encounter with the Lion, how she learns that he is good but not safe. After drawing from her a penitent confession for her foolish showing off, Aslan forgives Jill and assigns to her a task to be shared with Eustace. They are to find a lost prince in Narnia and bring him to his father's house. The Lion gives her four signs to guide their quest: (1) As soon as Eustace arrives in Narnia, he will meet a dear friend, whom he must greet immediately. (2) They must travel north out of Narnia until they reach the ruined city of the ancient giants. (3) In that city they will find writing on stone that will give them direction. (4) They will know the lost prince in that he will be the first person they meet on the entire journey who will ask them to do something in the name of Aslan.

The Lion has Jill repeat the signs until she gets them right. He stresses the importance of remembering them, telling her to say them over and over and let nothing turn her from following them. He warns that the signs will not look like she and Eustace expect them to look. They must pay no attention to appearances. With the instructions complete, Aslan sends Jill to join Eustace in Narnia.

BEGINNING THE QUEST

The children miss the first sign. The dear friend Eustace meets is King Caspian. But Eustace does not recognize him because in

Narnian time many decades have passed since the *Dawn Treader* voyage. Caspian is now an old man. The children get help from the owls, who send them to Puddleglum the marsh-wiggle—a creature somewhat between a jumping frog and a scarecrow. Lewis modeled Puddleglum's character after his gardener, F. W. Paxford, "an inwardly optimistic, outwardly pessimistic, dear, frustrating, shrewd countryman of immense integrity."[2] Many readers find Puddleglum to be the most endearing of all Narnian characters after Aslan.

With Puddleglum's help Eustace and Jill follow the second sign and journey north out of Narnia. They reach the ruined city of the giants in a bitterly cold windstorm. The children's determination to find shelter causes them to miss the third sign. This leads to near disaster. The giants imprison them and plan to eat them. But looking out the upper-floor castle window, they see the words *Under Me* written in huge letters that are actually trenches in the stone pavement below. They realize that they walked inside those very trenches as they fought the wind. Before we address the meaning of this sign, let's pause to look at what C. S. Lewis is telling us.

Like Eustace and Jill, we are given signs—directions to follow that lead us to accomplish God's purpose. We find those directions in their most visible, concrete, and institutional form, in the Bible. Aslan's admonition to Jill to remember the signs echoes the language of an Old Testament command. The Lion tells her: "Say them to yourself when you wake in the morning and when you lie down at night, and when you wake in the middle of the night. And whatever strange things may happen to you, let nothing turn your mind from following the signs."[3]

Shortly before the Israelites entered their promised land, Moses urged them to remember all the Lord's commands: "And these words which I command you today shall be in your heart. You shall teach them diligently to your children, and shall talk of them when you sit in your house, when you walk by the way, when you lie down, and when you rise up."[4] The idea is to make God's commands so familiar that they become an ingrained second nature.

God's directions to us take other forms as well. For example, he often speaks through our consciences. In *The Lion, the Witch and the Wardrobe* the faun Tumnus is about to betray Lucy to the White Witch. But his conscience prods him to do the right thing, and he escorts her back to the lamppost. Regardless of the form of God's directions, two characteristics are always common to them. First, they always move us closer to his will. And second, we often misinterpret them because we fail to see them clearly.

WHY DOES GOD BOTHER?

Why didn't Aslan just rescue the prince himself instead of depending on a couple of blundering kids and a silly-looking marsh-wiggle? Why does God move *us* to do his will when a mere word from him would get the job done? We've already uncovered some of the answer in chapter 4. We were designed to be "little gods"—his deputies on this earth. That's what it means to be created in his image. The Fall crippled the image, but we are still the same kinds of beings he created us to be. And he still pays us that compliment of allowing us to be movers and shakers. Our actions still have meaning and make a difference. As Lewis wrote, "He seems to do nothing of Himself which He can possibly delegate to His creatures. He commands us to do slowly and blunderingly what He could do perfectly and in the twinkling of an eye."[5]

No doubt it would be easier for him to do it himself. It's easier for a mother to cook dinner herself than to guide her young children in tossing the salad, peeling the potatoes, and setting the table. But she delights in the salad, no matter how raggedly the lettuce and peppers are sliced. She delights in the table in spite of the puddles of tea and the awkwardly folded napkins. She knows that unless she gives her children instructions and lets them help, they will never develop into what they were meant to be.

LOOKING FOR CLARITY

Why are God's instructions so often unclear and hard to interpret? Aslan explains it to Jill this way:

> Here on the mountain I have spoken to you clearly: I will not often do so down in Narnia. Here on the mountain, the air is clear and your mind is clear; as you drop down into Narnia, the air will thicken. Take great care that it does not confuse your mind. And the signs which you have learned here will not look at all as you expect them to look, when you meet them there.[6]

Every Christian can attest to the truth of Aslan's warning. We have all experienced just how hard it often is to know the signs, to see God's will clearly, and to be confident that we understand it. And this is a great mystery to many of us. Why aren't his directions always clear? Many of us agonize over options and microanalyze every event as a possible sign indicating what we should do in a given situation. *On my way to work the traffic lights were red at every intersection. Is God telling me to turn back and take a day off? Last night Brandon finally asked me to marry him, but my devotional reading this morning warned of deceit and lying tongues. Is God telling me something?* Why must we deal with such uncertainty? Why can't this all-knowing, all-powerful God of the universe tell us plainly and clearly exactly what he wants of us?

It's not God's fault; his voice is as clear as ever. The problem is that old dragon inside each of us. That fallen nature we inherited from Adam and Eve jams the signals. The Fall has sullied and distorted the true self God meant you and me to be, and the God of absolute truth has trouble making himself clear to creatures so out of kilter. It's as if our hearing is so impaired that no matter how loudly he shouts, we hear *no* when he says *go*.

But to be fair to ourselves, it's not all our fault. The Fall affects not only our souls and bodies but everything around us. Nature itself has suffered damage, and our entire environment now works against us. It tires us. It dulls our alertness. It obscures our vision of truth. Contending with the evil and chaos surrounding us distracts our attention and saps our clarity. When the clear truth of God descends into the polluted air of the Fall, its shape is dimmed and blurred.

That is why Aslan told Jill to remain alert for the signs when she entered Narnia. The air would thicken and her mind would be less clear. The children quickly discovered the truth of the warning, muffing the very first sign; Eustace did not recognize the aged Caspian. We find his error excusable. How could he possibly have known that this frail old king was the strong young Caspian who had commanded the voyage to the end of the world only a year before (in Eustace's time frame)? If the fog of the Fall had not dulled his mind, he might have figured it out. He knew that Narnian time did not flow parallel to earth time. He knew to be alert for a friend, and he knew the need to remain alert for the signs. But these considerations didn't jell in his mind, as they certainly would have in the mind of an unfallen boy.

How Can We Know?

Eustace, Jill, and Puddleglum miss the third sign although they are walking in the very trenches that formed the words they were searching for. When Aslan said they would find writing on stone, no doubt they pictured something like a cornerstone with words engraved on it. It never occurs to them that the letters might be deep enough to walk in. To make matters worse, they are in utter misery and near exhaustion from fighting a bitter wind. Again their failure seems understandable. The signs didn't look anything like they expected. Who could imagine the words would be written in trenches?

A similar kind of thing often happens to me. In a strange town I sometimes stop at a convenience store to ask for directions. The clerk will say something like, "Follow this road south. After you cross two railroad tracks, go through three stop signs, then take the next left. Soon you will see a trailer park. Take Highway 212 and exit after you pass the lake." I will likely get on the road south with no problem. But when I come to the railroad crossing, it will be a double track, where I expected a single. Did the clerk mean this double track to count as one? Or is this actually the two tracks? I move on and quickly pass through two of the three stop signs. I travel for miles but see no more. Finally I come to a stoplight. Did he say stop *sign* but mean stop*light*? I pass through the light and begin looking for the first left turn. Instead of a clear, ninety-degree turn, I come to a fork with a road veering to the left. Could this be the turn? Why didn't he call it a fork? I reach a trucking company parking lot filled with truck trailers. When the clerk said *trailer park*, I envisioned house trailers. Is this what he really meant? Once on Highway 212, I see a large cattle pond and wonder if this is the "lake" I was to pass.

Following God's will often presents similar problems. The signs are not what we expect, and we get muddled. God is creative. He is not boxed in by expectations. Our task is to remain open to whatever form his directions take.

Often the signs simply don't point in the way we want to go. In such cases we tend to confuse ourselves by rationalizing our way toward what we want to do, perhaps toward a less painful course. In *The Lion, the Witch and the Wardrobe*, after the children learn the fate of Tumnus, who has been captured by the White Witch, Susan wonders if they should continue into Narnia. "It doesn't seem particularly safe here and it looks as if it won't be much fun either,"[7] she says. Lucy insists they must go on because the faun is in danger and needs their help.

Many Christians consider comfort and safety a factor in deciding their course of action. But Lewis warns:

It is impossible to accept Christianity for the sake of finding comfort: but the Christian tries to lay himself open to the will of God, to do what God wants him to do. You don't know in advance whether God is going to set you to do something difficult or painful.[8]

We are simply to do what we're called to do.

We find a clear illustration of the rationalization process in Lewis's novel *Perelandra*. The hero Ransom has been sent to Venus, where he witnesses a diabolic creature tempting the unfallen first woman of that planet. He realizes that she will succumb unless something is done. He considers what he should do, always resisting the option that keeps pressing in on him. Maybe he has been sent to present the alternative argument. Or maybe to record the event for history. Or maybe just to do his best. But none of his rationalizations holds up. Finally the terrible truth overpowers his excuses: He has been sent to engage the hideous creature in mortal combat.

Often we fail to know God's will because, like Ransom, we resist the implications of what he requires. We confuse ourselves with rationalizations, blinding our hearts to the truth we don't want to face. And we become so good at self-deception that we don't even recognize the gyrations of our minds that bring it about.

Following the signs will not always lead us to comfort or safety. But it will always lead us to deeper joy. When Eustace, Jill, and Puddleglum reach the Underland where the prince is held, grim creatures capture them and march them through the dark caverns. But far from reacting in despair, the marsh-wiggle's spirits seem to be lifted. The reason, as he explains to Jill, is that "we're back on the right lines. We were to go under the Ruined City, and we *are* under it. We're following the instructions again."[9]

Good old Puddleglum! He seems pleased even in the hands of the enemy because he knows they are on the right track again. They are following the signs.

A Sign or a Coincidence?

Now we come to the greatest test that the three questing captives must face. The Underland creatures take them to the queen's palace. The queen is absent, and they meet a fine-looking young knight dressed in princely black. He does not believe in Narnia, Aslan, or the signs. He does not remember how he came to Underland. But he is deeply indebted to the queen for he is under a recurring enchantment, and she helps him through it. He explains that for one hour each night his mind is horribly changed, and he becomes wild, furious, and murderous. For that hour he is bound to a silver chair so that he cannot do the harm he threatens in his insane ravings.

Because the queen is not present, Puddleglum and the children contrive to stay with him for the hour. He extracts a promise that no matter how much he entreats, begs, or threatens, they will not loosen his bonds while the madness is upon him. They promise. Jill says, "There's nothing in the world he can say or do that'll make me change my mind."[10]

But when the "madness" comes upon the young man, he seems more sane than the queen's mindless toady he has been. He tells them that things are the opposite of what they have been told. The queen has captured and bewitched him, and it is only during the hour he is tied to the silver chair that he is really sane. Though his heartbreaking entreaties to free him shake the resolve of three observers, they hold to their promise. But suddenly he begs them in the name of the great Lion Aslan himself. Instantly they recognize the fourth sign: "You will know the lost prince . . . by this, that he will be the first person you have met in your travels who will ask you to do something in my name, in the name of Aslan."[11]

The observers don't know what to do. Could it be mere coincidence that the prince says the words of the sign? Could Aslan have meant for them to unbind a lunatic just because he happened to use those particular words? Could the evil queen have known of the signs and taught the knight the name of Aslan just to entrap them?

But what if this is the real sign? What was the point of learning them if they weren't going to obey them?

> "Oh, if only we knew!" said Jill.
>
> "I think we do know," said Puddleglum.
>
> "Do you mean you think everything will come right if we do untie him?" said Scrubb.
>
> "I don't know about that," said Puddleglum. "You see, Aslan didn't tell Pole what would happen. He only told her what to do. That fellow will be the death of us once he's up, I shouldn't wonder. But that doesn't let us off following the sign."[12]

The truth we must follow is usually simpler than all the complexities and rationalizations that keep us from recognizing it.

In spite of their uncertainties, Eustace, Jill, and Puddleglum release the young man—who is indeed Prince Rilian—and accomplish their task. Though it's not the prettiest of packages, the Lion's purpose is accomplished through his creatures. At the end of the story he greets the two children. Immediately they feel shame and inadequacy, thinking of their bumblings and failures. But the Lion, looking on them with infinite love, says, "Think of that no more. . . . You have done the work for which I sent you into Narnia."[13]

What a fine thing to hear! If we persevere in following the signs we are given, we can hear the same kind of commendation from our God: "Well done, good and faithful servant."[14] It is the same kind of commendation you give your children when they bring you breakfast in bed on your birthday. It doesn't matter about the runny eggs, the crumbling black bacon, the burnt toast, the tepid coffee full of grounds, or the mess you know awaits you in the kitchen. You are immensely pleased with the effort and the love that motivated it. You love what they intend. God is like that with us. He doesn't demand perfection we can't deliver. All he asks is that we follow the signs. And as Puddleglum says, "Aslan's instructions always work: there are no exceptions."[15]

CHAPTER 10

ASKING ASLAN
The Puzzle of Prayer

And when you put this horn to your lips and blow it, then,
wherever you are, I think help of some kind will come.
—FATHER CHRISTMAS, *THE LION, THE WITCH AND THE WARDROBE*

———◦•◦———

Prince Caspian and his counselors are desperate. They huddle within the caves inside the mound known as Aslan's How. Several companies of Telmarines surround them, determined to defeat Caspian and his small army of loyal Narnians so Caspian's uncle, Miraz, can retain the throne he has stolen. Things have not gone well for the young prince and his followers. They have made several sorties against the Telmarines, all of them disastrous in the face of the enemy's greater numbers. They need help badly, but they don't know where to turn.

"If your Majesty is ever to use the Horn," says the badger Trufflehunter, "I think the time has now come."[1] The loyal badger is speaking of the horn of Queen Susan, a relic from Narnia's golden days, many centuries ago. It is a magical horn given to her with the promise that in times of greatest need, she should blow it and help would come. Though many of his company do not believe in the horn, Caspian decides it is time to sound it.

As we read through the Narnia books, we find that every time the horn is blown help indeed comes. Aslan hears it and responds. He does not usually answer the call in his own person but sends help in the form of one of the children from our world. The sounding of the horn in Narnia is the same activity that we call prayer. And the answers come about in much the same way. Just as the horn in Narnia does not often bring Aslan himself, our prayers do not bring God himself, at least not in tangible form. God does much of his work in our world as Aslan does it in his. He sends others into our lives with the help we need.

The sounding of the horn, however, is not the only example of prayer in Narnia. Several Narnian characters make requests of Aslan in other ways and with varying results. Digory asks healing for his mother. The mouse Reepicheep asks for his lost tail to be restored. When the *Dawn Treader* is engulfed in the perpetual black night of the Dark Island where nightmares come true, Lucy whispers, "Aslan, if ever you loved us at all, send us help now."[2] Eustace Scrubb and Jill Pole, running from the school bullies, call to Aslan to deliver them into Narnia. Narnia's last king, Tirian, bound to a tree by the evil ape, calls out to Aslan for help. Each of these petitions is heard and answered.

In Narnia most prayers are answered in a direct and obvious way. But does it seem to you that prayer in our world is not quite so consistently effective? If you are like me, you have prayed many prayers that did not seem to be answered. Maybe you didn't get the needed raise, or the crucial sales deal fell through. The husband or wife you prayed for God to send never materialized. Or the dreaded thing you prayed to prevent happened anyway—you were caught in the company layoff; your finances collapsed; the biopsy report said malignant; the sick wife or husband or child died. Prayers don't seem always to work for any of us, no matter who we are. God did not remove a persistent affliction from the great apostle Paul even though he prayed fervently and repeatedly. Even the prayer of Jesus in Gethsemane was apparently denied. All this seems to fly in the face of the promise, "And whatever things you ask in prayer, believing, you will receive."[3] So does prayer work or doesn't it? Lewis hints at the answer to this question in Narnia.

A Matter of Timing

When Prince Caspian and his underground followers blow Susan's horn, days pass without the anticipated help coming, and their situation grows more desperate as the Telmarines close in. Nikabrik the dwarf tells the prince that the horn has failed. He should now turn to the dark powers for help. But Trufflehunter urges patience; he is confident that help is on the way. And it is. Unknown to them, it has already arrived in the form of the Pevensie children, who are listening just outside the door even as the debate rages.

Naturally we want our prayers answered immediately. That saves us stress and worry and puts no demands on our faith. But our experience is often the opposite. You pray for help to meet the financial crisis, and an unexpected check arrives on just the day you need it. You are deeply grateful, but you wonder why it could not have come a few days earlier to keep you from sweating it out. The very fact that we tend to sweat it out may indicate the reason for the delay. As we have explained in previous chapters, since the Fall humans have tended to trust first in themselves. God wants us to shift that trust to him. His timing in answering our prayers may be little lessons in trust. They show us that he is dependable. When we see the pattern repeating, we learn to relax in his care and quit worrying needlessly. He cares for the sparrows and assures us that we are worth immensely more to him than they are.[+]

There may be other reasons our prayers are not always answered immediately. The four Pevensie children are whisked into Narnia from an English railway station the moment Caspian blows the horn. Aslan gets them to Narnia immediately, but their late arrival at Caspian's camp is due to their own mistakes. God still uses us to do his work on earth even though our sin nature and foggy understanding hamper our effectiveness.

The Bible shows other reasons why answers to prayer can be delayed. In the book of Daniel we find an intriguing incident of conflict among angels. Chapter 9 relates Daniel's prayer for his people. Three weeks later an angel appears to him saying his words have been heard; the angel has been sent in answer. He explains his late arrival: He was delayed for twenty-one days by evil angels of Persia. He might have been delayed even further had not Michael the archangel come to his aid. Who knows what kinds of battles among invisible spirits may affect the delivery of God's answers to our prayers?

EXPECTATIONS VERSUS REALITY

Even when the answer to Caspian's horn does arrive, it is hardly what some of his supporters expect. When Trumpkin the loyal dwarf meets the Pevensies, he does not see how four children can really help Caspian in his dire situation. But he soon learns that the children are skilled warriors. And they are not the only help that's coming. Aslan is working behind the scenes to awaken an army of living trees to rout the Telmarines. Four children and sentient trees on the march are hardly the kind of help any of Caspian's people could have imagined.

There's an old story about a boy who fell from the roof of a two-story house. Immediately he cried, "God, save me!" An instant later he dangled in midair, his fall arrested. "Never mind, God," he said. "My pants just caught on Dad's flagpole hook." When the boy prayed, he expected the hand of God to catch him. When a seemingly small and ordinary hook saved him, he failed to see it as an answer to his prayer.

SELFISH PRAYERS

We sometimes hear it said that petitionary prayer is unworthy of a mature Christian, that truly spiritual prayers should focus on praise for God rather than requests from him. To continually ask him to meet our needs and wants seems more self-centered than God-centered because it indicates a lack of trust in God to give us what he knows we should have. This all has a noble and lofty ring to it, but as Lewis points out, it hardly reflects the pattern of prayer the New Testament presents. "The most unblushingly petitionary prayers are there recommended to us both by precept and example. Our Lord in Gethsemane made a petitionary prayer."[5] On another occasion Jesus taught his disciples a model prayer—a prayer filled with requests, not only for the advancement of God's kingdom, but also for their own needs, such as daily food, forgiveness, and deliverance from evil.[6]

Lewis follows that model and fills Narnia with petitionary prayers. When Aslan sends Digory and Polly on the back of the flying horse Fledge in quest of the silver apple, they stop for the night in a valley in the heart of the mountains. The children are hungry, and Digory wonders why no arrangement was made for their meals.

> "I'm sure Aslan would have, if you'd asked him," said Fledge.
>
> "Wouldn't he know without being asked?" said Polly.
>
> "I've no doubt he would," said the Horse. . . . "But I've a sort of idea he likes to be asked."[7]

It's as if Fledge has read the words of Jesus in the Sermon on the Mount: "For your Father knows the things you have need of before you ask Him."[8]

If God knows our needs before we ask, why does he want us to ask? I can see two reasons. First, it's a matter of alignment. God wants us to want what he knows we should have. He wants our minds to get in step with his and recognize our needs through his perspective. Our prayers show how closely we are aligned—or not. Second, God wants us to pray for what he wants to give so we will acknowledge him as the source of all we have. Prayer for our needs expresses our awareness of our continual dependence on him. And the more we pray and see how prayers are answered, including which are answered and which are not, the closer we come to the mind of God and learn to blend our wills with his.

The pattern of New Testament prayer shows that it is not selfish to desire what God knows you should have. Nor is it selfish to desire freedom from distress or pain. Distress and pain are evils, and it is right that we should want to be free of them. God wants us to have what is good for us, but many of our prayers go far beyond that. We Americans live in a society of unparalleled affluence where extreme luxury and ease have become the norm. The sleek model in the television commercial treats herself to the expensive perfume or clothing or automobile "because I deserve it." And we pick up the same attitude. Why shouldn't we have all the luxury, comfort, entertainment, transportation, money, oversized homes, lavish menus, and reshaped bodies as everyone else? We expect it, and those expectations creep—no, they *storm*—into our prayers. Such prayers treat God as the ultimate vending machine. We push the button of prayer and expect abundance to fall into the tray. "You ask and do not receive," wrote the church leader James, "because you ask amiss, that you may spend it on your pleasures."[9] Could this be one reason many of our prayers go unanswered?

IMPOSING OUR WILL ON GOD

Often our prayers are not pure requests made in faith but bargains with God not too different from Faust's bargain with the devil. The formula is basically this: "If you give me what I want now, I will serve you the rest of my life." Deathbed or battlefield promises follow the same pattern: "Get me through this, and I will give my life to you." Such prayers are not real commitments to God, but rather commitments to self—to having things arranged the way we want them. They are attempts to leverage God into giving us a thing we desperately want—now. Certainly the needs of a dying person or a soldier caught in gunfire are real and worth praying about. The problem is not the prayer but the condition added to it. *Let's make a deal, God; I want something from you, and you want something from me. You give me what I want, and I'll give you what you want.* It is a manipulative attempt to bend God's will to ours.

A deeper look into such prayers shows that we are not really giving God what we promise. The typical promise is quite extravagant—our very lives for the rest of our days. But the fact that the promise is conditional shows its true colors. We are not really putting our lives in God's hands; we are offering the self as an unwilling hostage in exchange for what we want. If God accepts the deal, we will take up religion—not from commitment to God but as payment due. If we were truly willing to give ourselves to God, we would do it without any condition.

Such conditional prayers are not always selfish in the sense that they are for one's own benefit. They may be for the life or healing of someone we love. Yet these prayers are selfish in that they do not fully trust God but rather trust in our own ability to pay for what we get—to meet the terms we offer. We are unwilling to trust God to do the right thing, so we must offer a deal.

The magician's nephew Digory desperately wants Aslan to heal his mother. When the Lion approaches him with the task we've already described, Digory "had for a second some wild idea of saying 'I'll try to help you if you'll promise to help my Mother,' but he realized in time that the Lion was not at all the sort of person one could try to make bargains with."[10] Digory submits and says a simple yes to Aslan's request and embarks on the difficult quest without condition.

IMPOSSIBLE ANSWERS

Many of our prayers may be simply impossible to answer, or impossible to answer without causing some other great harm. After Digory humbly accepts Aslan's charge to retrieve the silver apple from the wilds of the north, he does ask the Lion to heal his mother. Though he makes no conditions, he hopes Aslan will give him the healing apple. Aslan answers gently and tearfully:

I know. Grief is great. . . . But I have to think of hundreds of years in the life of Narnia. The Witch whom you have brought into this world will come back to Narnia again. But it need not be yet. It is my wish to plant in Narnia a tree that she will not dare to approach, and that tree will protect Narnia from her for many years.[11]

Sometimes one need must take precedence over another. The apple that could heal Digory's mother must be used to protect all Narnia.

We've all wondered how God handles the dilemma when the farmer who just planted prays for rain while his neighbor across the fence who needs to harvest prays for a dry spell. Or when two nations at war with each other both pray for victory. It is impossible, even for God, to reconcile mutually exclusive alternatives. But, you may say, doesn't the Bible tell us that all things are possible with God? Yes. All things that are possible at all are possible with God. But nothing that is innately impossible or self-contradictory is possible even for him. As Lewis explains:

> Meaningless combinations of words do not suddenly acquire meaning simply because we prefix to them the two other words, "God can." It remains true that all things are possible with God: the intrinsic impossibilities are not things but nonentities. It is no more possible for God than for the weakest of His creatures to carry out both of two mutually exclusive alternatives; not because His power meets an obstacle, but because nonsense remains nonsense even when we talk it about God.[12]

Nothing that contradicts God's own nature is possible with him. You cannot expect God to answer your prayer to zap a neighbor who doesn't mow his lawn, lets his dog run loose, and plays loud music at midnight, because God is love. Neither does he violate his own laws. He cannot make two plus two equal five because he made the rules of mathematics to be absolute and consistent, and he cannot violate them. Lucy, wanting to reverse the invisibility of the Dufflepuds, reads the spell that makes all things visible. Immediately Aslan appears. He tells her that her reading of the spell made him visible. She does not believe that anything she could do would have such an effect on him, but he assures her that it did. "Do you think I wouldn't obey my own rules?"[13]

God does not violate nature. His miracles are restorations of nature, not violations of it. Many of our prayers would require him to overturn the laws of nature to get us off the hook. If you keep taking rugged mountain trail-bike excursions on threadbare tires, don't bother asking God to keep you from having a flat. You can't deliberately challenge the laws of nature and ask him to spare you the consequences. He doesn't do that.

Of course we cannot always know when we are asking an impossible prayer. Like the child who asks for a pet unicorn, we may naively assume that possibilities exist where they do not. Our prayers must be like that of Jesus, "not as I will, but as You will."[14]

LARGER ANSWERS

We can see why some prayers are answered and some are not. If God denied the prayers of Jesus and the apostle Paul, we should be shamed by our own complaints that he does not always answer us. But wait! Perhaps the prayer of Jesus *was* answered. Let's take another look. Luke tells us that as he prayed, "an angel appeared to Him from heaven, strengthening Him."[15] And when we look again at Paul, we find that God did not ignore him either. The Lord told him, "My grace is sufficient for you, for My strength is made perfect in weakness."[16] God gave Paul a tremendous gift: his own strength to fill the apostle's weak spot, not only making him stronger but also displaying God's power in him. Neither Jesus nor Paul seemed to get the answers he wanted, yet each received answers much larger than he prayed for. God accomplished his purpose in them and at the same time addressed their request by giving them strength to bear the burden. In the long run God gave answers that met their needs—not in the way that spared them pain but in a way that accomplished a greater good.

Many of our prayers that seem to be ignored are answered in this way. Instead of removing the obstacle or the pain, God gives us the strength to overcome it or bear it. Rather than let us sink into atrophied weakness and fail to accomplish his greater purposes, he lets us bear the pain and gives us greater strength. Our suffering makes us more like him. It burns out of us all that is not eternal so that what is left can stand pure before him. Submitted prayer can be an instrument that blends our will with his. As C. S. Lewis's spiritual mentor George MacDonald says as a character in *The Great Divorce*, "There are only two kinds of people in the end: those who say to God, 'Thy will be done,' and those to whom God says, in the end. 'Thy' will be done.'"[17] God will not violate your will, but he urges you to do what you are made to do and submit your will to his and find supreme joy as a result. Prayer is an aid to aligning your will with his.

CHAPTER 11

ASLAN ON THE MOVE
The Mystery of Providence

I have now lived a hundred and nine winters in this world and
have never yet met any such thing as Luck.

—THE HERMIT OF THE SOUTHERN MARCH, *THE HORSE AND HIS BOY*

The Horse and His Boy, perhaps more than any other Narnia book, shows the workings of what Christians call providence. As the story begins, a wealthy Tarkaan comes to the squalid hut of the poor fisherman Arsheesh and wants to buy his boy, Shasta. Shasta, listening through a crack in the wall, hears the entire conversation. At first Arsheesh tries to pretend the boy is his own, but the Tarkaan is not fooled. Shasta's fair skin shows him to be from the north, whereas the fisherman, like all Calormenes, is dark skinned. Arsheesh relents and tells the dignitary how the boy came to be in his care. On a given night he could not sleep, and he left his bed and wandered toward the sea. At that moment a boat washed ashore carrying the body of a man, who had apparently just died of hunger, and an infant boy weakened from lack of food.

The Tarkaan offers fifteen crescents for Shasta. Arsheesh is offended. "Fifteen! For the prop of my old age and the delight of my eyes! Do not mock my gray beard, Tarkaan though you be. My price is seventy."[1] So the haggling begins, and young Shasta knows he is about to be sold. But what he has heard excites him. He has never felt at home with Arsheesh, and he has often felt drawn to the north and longed to know what lay there. He slips out to where the Tarkaan's horse is stabled and wonders aloud what he should do. Unable to come up with a plan, he wishes that the horse could talk. "But I can," the horse responds, to Shasta's great surprise. It is a talking horse named Bree, kidnapped from Narnia. The horse and the boy decide to escape together and head north across the desert to Narnia.

Webster defines *providence* as "divine guidance or care." The word generally refers to the workings of God to bring about his will in the earth. Miracles also accomplish God's will, but Christians generally distinguish providence from miracles in this way; providence is God's use of *natural* means to achieve his purpose while in miracles he modifies or suspends the normal workings of nature. We understand Jesus' turning water into wine to be a miracle. We see the growing of the plant to shield Jonah from the sun not as a miracle but as providence, because it came about by natural means.

In each instance God was actively at work. In miracles, his hand is obvious, spectacular, and visible. In providence, we think of him as keeping behind the curtain, pulling strings, flipping switches, making adjustments, fine-tuning events, and nudging us toward the action he wants. Such work is often unrecognized or even hidden because it is camouflaged within nature. And because it is hidden, we fail to see how incessantly he works to move us in the right direction and accomplish his purpose in our lives.

Of course in a story like *The Horse and His Boy*, providence becomes obvious because the being behind the curtain is identified for us. For example, as the boy Shasta and the warhorse Bree escape the fisherman's hut, two other escapees—the young Calormene girl Tarkheena Aravis and the Narnian talking mare Hwin—also ride into the night toward Narnia. Aslan has reasons for wanting the four to travel together, so he roars to frighten the horses and their riders toward each other. Later, while waiting alone at night for the rendezvous at the desert tombs, Shasta is caught between his fear of ghouls from the tombs and jackals approaching from the desert. A huge Lion chases away the jackals and a large Cat comforts him as he waits out the night. In the last stages of their grueling journey to warn Narnia of a Calormene invasion, the two horses think they are spent and fail to muster up the effort required to complete their task. A Lion appears behind them and frightens them into an unprecedented burst of speed. After delivering the warning, Shasta rides alone across the perilous mountain pass into Narnia. An invisible presence walks by his side, protecting him on the narrow ledges. At this point Aslan speaks to Shasta and reveals himself as the one who has been his protector throughout the journey and throughout his entire life.

Some of Aslan's nudgings seem "providential." Some seem more like miracles. In Narnia there is often little distinction. The overriding idea is that Aslan is always on the move, and he is the directive power behind all that is accomplished.

PROVIDENCE OR CHANCE?

Christians differ widely over just how involved God is in the affairs of humans. Some believe he is only minimally involved, allowing chance and circumstance to play themselves out largely at random. Lewis's own conviction was that God is highly involved in everything that happens. "If God directs the course of events at all then he directs the movement of every atom at every moment; 'not one sparrow falls to the ground' without that direction."[2] His conviction of the extent of God's involvement in the universe shows up throughout the Narnia stories, and it is succinctly expressed by one character in *The Horse and His Boy*. After the horses and children ride into the compound of the hermit of the Southern March, the hermit attends to Aravis's wounded back and tells her the scratches are neither deep nor dangerous.

"I say!" said Aravis. "I have had luck."

"Daughter," said the Hermit, "I have now lived a hundred and nine winters in this world and have never yet met any such thing as Luck."[3]

Lewis illustrates this principle in *The Silver Chair* when Prince Rilian, still under the spell of the Green Lady, hears that Puddleglum and the two children came into the Underland because they followed a sign saying "Under Me." The prince laughs and says they have been deceived. The sign could not have been meant for them because it was part of a longer quotation engraved into the stone centuries ago. And it referred not to the location of the Underland but to the dominion of an ancient king. Time eroded the quotation, leaving only those two words. The rational explanation dismays the children, but Puddleglum says, "Don't you mind him. . . . There *are* no accidents. Our guide is Aslan; and he was there when the giant king caused the letters to be cut, and he knew already all things that would come of them; including *this*."[4]

PROVIDENCE VERSUS FREE WILL

Aslan's centuries of planning to create the "Under Me" sign for Puddleglum and the children illustrate the extreme complexity that must be involved in meshing God's activity with humanity's free will, especially since the Fall. In Eden there was no tension between God's purpose and our free will. Adam and Eve were totally submitted to him, and so his purpose and theirs were one. Since the Fall we often exercise our free will in opposition to God's will. He will not prevent the exercise of our free will, and yet he intends to see his purpose ultimately accomplished. How can he do both? How can God accomplish his will on earth and in our lives and yet allow our free will?

Lewis finds the explanation in the relationship of time to eternity. God does not progress along a time line as we do. In *Mere Christianity* Lewis helps us to picture this idea by representing time as a pencil line on a blank sheet of paper. The paper is eternity, a greater reality containing all of time. God, living in eternity (the paper), has free access to any segment of time (the line) that he chooses to attend to. Therefore he can observe all of time at will; the past, the present, and the future are equally present to him. "What we call 'tomorrow' is visible to him in just the same way as what we call 'today,'" Lewis says. "He does not 'foresee' you doing things tomorrow; He simply sees you doing them."[5]

God observes the future event as a fixed reality while in no way being the cause of it. In that sense he is a passive spectator just as you are when you review an event in the past. This means, as Lewis explains in his book *Miracles*, that God can look at what you will do as if you have already done it. And he can create a miracle or design an act of nature to complement or counter your act and bring about his purpose.

Believing this to be the way God works, Lewis makes no real distinction between what we call providence and the normal workings of nature. God built "providence" into nature at the beginning. God's ability to see the future as an eternal present allowed him to take into account all prayers yet to be prayed and set nature in motion at the outset in a way that brought about the necessary natural events to address all needs at their proper time.[6] To answer a farmer's prayer for rain, God must either perform a miracle or, as Lewis suggests, build into the stream of nature at the beginning all the causative movements required to have a rain cloud in position on the day it's needed. The concept is staggering, but it becomes at least comprehensible when we remember that God is outside of time, and his foreknowledge allows him to have that farmer's prayer (and all other prayers) before him at the moment of creation.

The writing of fiction has helped me to understand the meshing of man's free will and God's sovereignty. I created a set of characters, outlined a story, and gave each character a role in accomplishing the end I had in mind. As I began writing, however, I found, as novelists often do, that the characters seemed to take on a life of their own.[7] They wanted to depart from my plan and go off in their own directions. I saw two ways of handling the rebellion: Either I could force the characters to do exactly what I had created them to do, or I could let them follow their own inclinations and take the story out of my hands. I didn't much like either option. If I forced the characters to remain in the grooves I had designed for them, I knew I would end up with what critics call "cardboard characters." They would seem artificial and puppetlike because I would not be able to hide the strings I was pulling to force them to my will. On the other hand, I thought I had a pretty good plot with a satisfying conclusion, and I was reluctant to let these contrary characters ruin the happy destiny I had planned for them.

So I followed a third alternative. I let the characters do what they wanted. I allowed them to follow paths I had not set them on. I even let them make bad choices that I could have prevented. At the same time, I was determined to see my plot accomplished. So I added people and events to the story to head my heroes off when they went astray. I gave them mentors to show them paths, obstacles to divert their attention, and even disasters to stop them cold when nothing else would work.

Lewis illustrates some of the intricacies of providence by showing how a novelist might create a single disaster to accomplish several of his ends at once. One character in the story needs to be killed off; his daughter needs to be kept out of London; the hero needs to recover that woman's love; and another character needs a moral shock to shatter his conceit. The author solves it all with a train wreck. The accident kills the father, keeps the daughter away from London, the hero rescues the girl, and the conceited character's negligence caused the accident. Although the characters board the train to accomplish their own purposes, the author thwarts their plans to accomplish his, using an event that does not violate their free will. Lewis knew the illustration to be imperfect, but he hoped that "the example may suggest how Divine ingenuity could so contrive the physical 'plot' of the universe as to provide a 'providential' answer to the needs of innumerable creatures."[8]

Of course these illustrations do not address the extreme complexity of God working within events to bring about his will simultaneously in the lives of billions of people, all fallen, and all exercising free will. Facing such an enormity, we have to punt and ascribe the prodigious feat to the omnipotence of God. But I hope they help us to see, even if dimly, how our free will and his sovereignty are not mutually exclusive.

PROVIDENCE IN OUR WORLD

Narnia shows how providence can change our evil or bumbling acts into good. After failing to read the "Under Me" sign and enter the Underland, Puddleglum and the two children run for their lives when the giants return and find them escaping. They duck into a hole beneath the step of a stone stairway and find themselves sliding downward on scree in the darkness. At the end of their fall, they are where Aslan wants them to be—in the Underland.[9]

One of the most striking examples of God bringing good out of evil is the Old Testament account of Joseph. The eleventh of twelve boys, Joseph was his father's favorite. His jealous brothers sold him into slavery in Egypt and deceived their father into believing the boy had been killed. In Egypt Joseph rose by his own diligence, integrity, and a series of providential occurrences to become prime minister. Years later when the brothers came to Egypt to buy food for their famine-starved families, they were terrified to learn that the man they had to deal with was Joseph. But Joseph reassured them, "Do not therefore be grieved or angry with yourselves because you sold me here; for God sent me before you to preserve life."[10]

So who really put Joseph in Egypt? The evil brothers or a good God? The answer is both. Does this mean that God caused the brothers to hate Joseph and sell him as a slave? Of course not. It means that he knew what they would do of their own volition and prepared other events to bring from their evil the good he intended. His providence does not extend to causing a person to do evil in violation of his free will.

But wait, you may say, didn't God cause Pharaoh to do evil by hardening his heart against releasing the Israeli slaves at the demand of Moses? Not really. If you place a stick of butter and a lump of wet clay in the sun, the heat will melt the butter and harden the clay. But it's not the sun's *fault* that the clay hardens; it's just what that particular substance naturally does when exposed to sunlight. Pharaoh's heart was such that exposure to God would cause it to harden. He chose the kind of heart he would have, and he made his own decisions by his own free will.[11]

God hates evil and is never the cause of it. Nevertheless, he uses it for his own purposes. Everyone is an instrument in his hands, either voluntarily and willingly or involuntarily in spite of his intentions. God will complete the story according to his plot, and all the characters will bring about the conclusion he wants. It's for us to choose whether to be evil characters who get our comeuppance in the end or good ones who, like Shasta, win the throne that is ours to claim.

It is not uncommon for God to use harrowing experiences to turn us off one path and in a new direction. The roar of the lions at night frightens the two horses, Bree and Hwin, into altering their courses so they will meet each other and travel together. The result is that the horses can help each other on the journey, taking advantage of Bree's strength and Hwin's humble but judicious common sense. It also introduces Shasta to his future bride, Aravis. But the experience is terrifying, because all of them think the lions in the darkness are mortal dangers.

PROVIDENCE AND PAIN

The queen of Underland has thrown a mind-dulling powder into the fire and, playing her lute, she has almost lulled Puddleglum, Eustace, and Jill into believing that her drab world of darkness is all that exists and that the bright land of Narnia with its golden Lion is only a beautiful dream. But Puddleglum retains just enough sense to realize the danger. He stomps out the fire with his bare foot, burning himself severely. The pain clears the marsh-wiggle's head to where he knows the truth and is able to act on it. Sometimes a mere scare won't do the job, and it takes pain to get our attention. We become lulled by the comforts and philosophies of this underland we live in—the Shadowlands, as Lewis called our world—and forget the bright promise of heaven. Sometimes nothing but pain will clear our heads and shake us awake.

Writer Sheldon Vanauken and his beautiful young wife, Davy, had the ideal marriage. They were totally wrapped up in each other, and their love was their fortress against everything the world could throw at them. Vanauken was devastated when Davy died, but later he realized, partly as a result of a series of letters from C. S. Lewis, that her death was a "severe mercy" to both of them.[12] Their devotion to each other had become an exclusive thing that threatened to crowd out their love of God. It was necessary that they be separated so that both would find God.

Joni Eareckson Tada is paralyzed from the neck down as the result of a diving accident in her late teens. Now in her fifties, her remarkable life has influenced thousands for the Lord. She says she now realizes that the horrible accident headed her toward God's light, and she would not undo it if she could. Does this mean that Joni likes being paralyzed? Certainly not. She dreams of a heaven where her body will be restored. But she knows her paralysis is another severe mercy.

We've all had experiences in which a doctor's diagnosis, the loss of a job, an automobile accident, or a narrow escape in a storm or disaster brought us up short and made us face realities we had avoided. Diseases, accidents, and storms are all evils, but they often clear our heads of the fog and clutter that obscure simple truths. Painful or frightening though they are, these obstacles become blessings when God uses them to clarify our thinking. As Lewis says, "God whispers to us in our pleasures, speaks in our conscience, but shouts in our pains: It is God's megaphone to rouse a deaf world."[13]

God's Direction

Providence does not necessarily involve pain. In fact, most of God's direction in our lives appears perfectly benign, as the Narnian stories show us in the following two of many examples:

The Pevensie children have been told to stay out of the way of the guide when she gives tours of Professor Kirke's mansion. Attempting to comply, they find themselves strangely thwarted in every direction except the room with the wardrobe. When the tour enters that room, they are forced to hide inside the wardrobe, and thus all four make their first trip together into Narnia. Aslan's plan called for them to come into Narnia at that time, and he accomplished it through the tour guide's unwitting "herding" of them.

Beleaguered Narnian defenders under King Tirian make their last stand backed up against a white rock with enemies all around. They are without food and water until a trickle comes out of the rock, refreshing them much as it did Moses and the Hebrews in the Sinai desert.

Lewis relates one experience of his own in which he felt a continuing urge to get a haircut on a given day. On reaching the barbershop, he found that the barber had been praying that he would come on that day to help him with a particular problem that could not have waited.[14] You may have experienced similar occurrences in which it seems that some greater hand somehow prodded you to do a given thing at a given moment. Often we see such things more clearly when we look back and notice, to our wonder, how a single incident affected the course of our lives from that moment on, or how a certain pivotal thing happened because a particular set of choices and occurrences led up to it.

THE REST OF THE STORY

At the end of Shasta's story, we see how all the individual instances of Aslan's providence fit into a larger plan. Shasta is recognized as Cor, the lost prince of Archenland and heir to the crown of that kingdom. The entire sequence of events—the escape of the boat bearing the baby from the attacked ship, the fisherman Arsheesh's sleepless night, the visit of the Tarkaan and his Narnian horse Bree, all the way down to the meeting of Shasta and his father, King Lune—was orchestrated to bring Shasta to his throne and to his queen (for he later married Aravis).

Once we submit to God's direction, we find great comfort and security in the knowledge that we are guided, protected, and watched over by an all-powerful being who loves us with a tenacious and over-powering love. Narnia shows us such a world, and Narnia is a picture of our own. Shasta's story is our story. We sense that we are not natives to our country, and we long for another that we sense but cannot see. We are destined to be kings and queens of a beautiful kingdom. But powers beyond our control have alienated us far from our true country and placed us in danger of being sold to evil powers. By aligning ourselves with others escaping slavery, we can support and encourage one another as we travel toward our true country, where we will be welcomed as sons and daughters of the King. As we journey, God is at work in and around us, helping, directing, prodding, and protect-ing. His providence is his love at work.

CHAPTER 12

FLYING YOUR FLAG
The Committed Company

You haven't yet found out whether I want to go back. I don't. I
want to stay with you—if you will have me. I've been looking
for people like you all my life.

—CASPIAN, *PRINCE CASPIAN*

———◆◆◆———

Who doesn't long for a place to belong, to be on the inside
where there's good company, good conversation, and goodwill?
We hate being outsiders. We want to be part of the group, to fit
in, to be accepted, to enjoy camaraderie and fellowship with others devoted to a common and significant cause. Prince Caspian
finds such a company, and it closely resembles something you
may recognize.

As the book *Prince Caspian* opens, King Miraz the usurper sits
on the throne of Narnia. He has murdered the rightful king and,
being childless himself, raised his nephew, Prince Caspian, to succeed him. But when the king fathers a son, Caspian is an obvious
threat to the child's succession, and he must flee for his life. The
young prince mounts his horse and rides out into the night.

Reaching the wilds of Narnia, Caspian discovers the "Old
Narnians," animals, dwarfs, centaurs, giants, and other creatures
who must live in hiding from the Telmarine usurpers. With Caspian
the rightful king among them, the Old Narnians gather in council

and decide the time is right to wage war against Miraz and regain the throne. They blow the ancient horn of Queen Susan, which brings the help of the four kings and queens of Narnia's golden age and also the help of Aslan, in the form of a militant, marching forest. After winning the battle, the Old Narnians celebrate with feasting, dancing, and fine fellowship around a great bonfire. "The best thing of all about this feast," Lewis writes, "was that there was no breaking up or going away."[1]

In Prince Caspian's Narnia, C. S. Lewis presents a fellowship that has many attributes of the Christian church. In fact, I'm convinced that he meant Narnia to be a picture of the church. More than once in other works he notes that Christians live in "enemy occupied territory." Our situation is the same as Caspian's. We are the rightful rulers of the earth, but a usurper has stolen our kingdom and set himself up as the "ruler of this world." Now we are soldiers in a resistance movement led by a commander from outside our world who has promised to reestablish us on our throne.

The citizens of Narnia share many other characteristics with the church. Narnia in its finest moments is a fellowship of free creatures committed to the well-being of one another and to their King—the Emperor-beyond-the-Sea and his Son Aslan. Narnia exists as a kingdom apart. Though always threatened and sometimes troubled by cruel enemies such as the Telmarines, the White Witch, the Green Lady, and the infidel Calormenes, Narnians maintain their commitment to one another and their King. Like Narnia, the church exists in a world dominated by enemies. It is often under attack from governments, naturalistic philosophies, and hostile religions. Church members hold together in an attitude of love, loyalty, courtesy, and support, sharing both their good things and their burdens as they face threats and attacks from without. Let's look closer at specific incidents in Narnia that show the parallels.

Love, Commitment, and Mutual Suffering

Love and mutual respect in Narnia often reveal themselves as simple courtesy and kindness. When Prince Caspian first meets the Old Narnians, he is not hungry at all, but he accepts a honeycomb from a bear and a nut from a squirrel rather than hurt their feelings. In a similar incident, Lucy offers her dainty handkerchief to the giant Rumblebuffin to wipe the sweat from his face after he has destroyed the gate of the White Witch's castle. Though the handkerchief is too tiny to be of any use, the giant kindly praises it as he wipes his brow with it. One of the first laws of love in Narnia as well as in the church is simple courtesy and kindness. Such sensitivity shows empathy, respect, and care for the feelings of others.

In the battle with the Telmarines, the valiant mouse Reepicheep loses his tail. The tail is a thing of pride for Narnian mice, and rather than see one of their own suffer humiliation, the other mice stand ready to cut off their own tails if Reepicheep's cannot be restored. In Narnia, as in the church, when one member hurts, all hurt with him and willingly share his pain and humiliation.

I've already mentioned the incident in *The Magician's Nephew* where Digory and Polly, on their quest for the silver apple, realize they have no food. Digory encourages Polly to use her magic ring to return to London and get food for herself. He must stick to the task he has been assigned. Polly, however, will not go. She refuses to leave Digory alone, and he deeply appreciates her loyalty. In trying to send Polly home for food, Digory thinks not of himself but of her, even though he knows anything might happen to prevent her return. Polly thinks not of herself but of Digory, sticking by him on his formidable task in spite of her hunger. It's the kind of sacrificial care and concern for one another that is characteristic of true Narnians and true Christians. As the apostle Paul wrote, "Bear one another's burdens, and so fulfill the law of Christ."[2]

A Safe Place to Be Transparent

In *The Voyage of the Dawn Treader*, after recovering from his terrible experience as a dragon, Eustace Scrubb realizes he has treated his shipmates horribly and confesses to Edmund: "I'd like to apologize. I'm afraid I've been pretty beastly." "That's all right," replies Edmund. "Between ourselves, you haven't been as bad as I was on my first trip to Narnia. You were only an ass, but I was a traitor."[3] On his second trip to Narnia, Eustace and his schoolmate Jill Pole are about to flee for their lives through the collapsing Underland. The two children take a moment and confess to each other. "Sorry I've been a funk and so ratty," says Eustace. "And I'm sorry I've been such a pig," replies Jill.[4]

Notice the kinds of apologies the children make. Eustace did not say, "I'm sorry *if* I was a funk and ratty." Those if-based apologies so commonly heard are not really apologies at all. Instead they show resistance to acknowledging wrongdoing and insinuate that the real problem is the oversensitivity of the offended party. "I'm sorry *if* I hurt you" implies, *You really should not have felt hurt by what I did. If you do feel offended, it's due to your own overreaction.* There is none of this in our Narnian friends' apologies. They admit the wrong outright and take full responsibility for offending. It's what a real confession ought to be.

Self-image is the problem of the horse Bree. He, the great warhorse, has galloped away in terror while the peasant boy Shasta has shown marvelous courage by standing between Aravis and the Lion. Bree broods alone, and no one can comfort him. Finally he tells Aravis that he is shamed by his cowardice. His admission is not a confession, however, but a wallowing in grief over the loss of his self-image as a courageous warhorse. Aravis confesses to Bree her own mistreatment of Shasta. She, the highborn Calormene Tarkheena, has been snubbing the boy and looking down on him as a mere peasant, though he turns out to be the best of them all. She wisely says, "I think it would be better to stay and say we're sorry than to go back to Calormen." Aravis has the right idea. Make your confession; get the shameful thing out of your system and into the open. But stay in the fellowship; don't go back to the past you have escaped. This kind of confession acknowledges the truth, faces it, and deals with it so one can be healed. But the horse cannot accept her advice. "It's all very well for you," says Bree. "You haven't disgraced yourself. But I've lost everything."

The hermit, who has approached unnoticed, responds,

My good Horse, you've lost nothing but your self-conceit. . . . You're not quite the great horse you had come to think, from living among poor dumb horses. Of course you were braver and cleverer than them. You could hardly help being that. It doesn't follow that you'll be anyone very special in Narnia. But as long as you know you're nobody very special, you'll be a very decent sort of Horse, on the whole.[5]

No One Is More Equal than Another

The hermit tells Bree that nobody is special in Narnia. Actually, this means that everybody is special in Narnia. All are free and equal. All are treated as if they were of supreme importance. There is no hierarchy of value that places one type of being above another or makes one class of creature inferior to the others. So when Shasta (now Prince Cor) brings Bree, Hwin, and Aravis into Archenland, King Lune comes out of his castle gate to greet them. After meeting the Calormene girl, he "turned to Hwin and Bree and was just as polite to them as to Aravis, and asked them a lot of questions about their families and where they had lived in Narnia before they had been captured."[6] The king thinks nothing of treating rational horses as his equals.

Narnia gives us a picture of the supreme value and equality before God that exists in the church, where "there is neither Jew nor Greek, there is neither slave nor free, there is neither male nor female; for you are all one in Christ Jesus."[7] In the church we see a deeper truth about one another that shows through our differences in race, status, wealth, sex, or ability. We see the one thing that is common to us all: that we are created in the image of God. As Lewis says:

> There are no ordinary people. You have never talked with a mere mortal. Nations, cultures, arts, civilisations—these are mortal, and their life is to ours as the life of a gnat. . . . Next to the Blessed Sacrament itself, your neighbour is the holiest object presented to your senses.[8]

Not only do we see God's image in one another, we also see the vulnerabilities and weaknesses that mar the image. Dealing with this darker side does not cause us to shun or turn away from others but rather to recognize in the mirror of our neighbors our own fallen condition and how desperately we need others to keep ourselves on track. As the Lion tells Caspian, "You come of the Lord Adam and the Lady Eve. And that is both honor enough to erect the head of the poorest beggar, and shame enough to bow the shoulders of the greatest emperor on earth."[9]

In the church, as in Narnia, no one is greater than anyone else. All are sinners. All face more temptation than they can handle alone, and all need the help of others in overcoming it. Confession lays one's weakness on the table and allows others to help both in watching for temptations and resisting them. It's the Alcoholics Anonymous idea. We're all in the same boat. Let's be honest and call ourselves by our right name. We are sinners. That means we are all, like alcoholics, addicts to sin in general and each to some sin in particular. Let's frankly admit to one another our weaknesses so we can face them openly and support one another when we cannot resist alone. That is exactly what the church is about.

We Christians often miss this point. We act as if we have it all together, failing to admit that we are addicted "sin-aholics." Church gatherings sometimes become showplaces for the masks of goodness we wear to hide that truth. And nonbelievers respond to the masks by labeling us as hypocrites. Both members and nonmembers misunderstand what the church is all about. As someone has aptly put it, the church is not a showplace for saints; it is a hospital for sinners. It's not a place for good people to strut their stuff but a place for forgiven people to help each other draw closer to God. Christians, like Narnians, are far from perfect. We have turned to God, and he has stripped off the dragon skin, but we still slip back into dragon mode. When these slips occur, we confess to each other, borrow strength from each other, and face life again.

VIVE LA DIFFÉRENCE

When Aslan sings his creation song and the animals emerge from the earth, each begins immediately to act according to its own nature. The moles dig their way out. The dogs come out barking. Bees head for the flowers as if they haven't a second to lose. Feline creatures first wash the dirt from their fur then sharpen their claws on trees.[10] Each creature is made to function differently from all the others. And each function is valuable to the whole, with each animal doing its specialized part.

These ingrained creature specialties hold true throughout the *Chronicles*, and often we can see exactly how each contributes to the well-being of all. When Aslan orders the animals to take up certain positions before marching into battle with the White Witch, a sheepdog sorts them into their proper order. When the Lion wants crowns for King Frank and Queen Helen, dwarfs, expert in metalcraft, rush to the task as moles dig for precious stones to set in the crowns. Dwarfs and moles also do what they do best in digging out Eustace, Jill, Puddleglum, and Prince Rilian when they reach the surface of the earth from the Underland. When Prince Caspian needs a messenger to meet the ancient kings and queens of Narnia, who could be better than Pattertwig the squirrel, considering his ability to stay in trees and get through enemy country without being caught? All these creatures function according to their individual natures, and the specialized work of each is vital to the whole.

We have in these individual specialties another picture of the Christian church. Paul tells us that our varying abilities enrich the whole. He compares the church to a human body and explains that each of our specialties is as vital to a healthy organism as that of a foot, a hand, or an eye to the body. A body cannot function if all its parts are the same: "If the whole body were an eye, where would be the hearing?"[11]

Father Christmas gives specialized gifts to three of the Pevensie children. To Peter he gives a sword and shield; to Susan a bow, arrows, and the magic horn; and to Lucy a vial of healing liquid and a dagger.[12] Throughout the books the children use these gifts to help Narnians in trouble and to accomplish Aslan's purposes. Paul tells us that the Holy Spirit gives Christians specialized gifts for the same purpose. "Having then gifts differing according to the grace that is given to us, let us use them," he urges. Then he goes on to list several specific gifts that God gives us to meet the needs of the body—prophecy, ministry, teaching, exhorting, giving, leading, and showing mercy.[13] When all these specialties are properly and lovingly employed, the church is a healthy, efficiently functioning body.

But things do not always work so smoothly. Sometimes these differences meant for good can cause confusion or dissention, even when exercised with the best of intentions. When the Old Narnians gather with Prince Caspian for the council to decide their course of action, creatures of all types attend—bears, dwarfs, badgers, hares, hedgehogs, satyrs, mice, owls, centaurs, a raven, and a giant. The proposals are as varied as the creatures making them. Bears want to have a feast before the council. The mice think the council is a waste of time; they want to storm Miraz's castle immediately. The chattering squirrels say they can talk and eat at the same time. The moles propose throwing up defensive entrenchments. The fauns want a solemn dance before beginning anything. The raven wants to make a speech. Only Caspian's authority brings order to the wildly diverse group.

THE BODY AND THE HEAD

Submission to authority is the only way Caspian's diverse army could be effective, and it's the only way the church can be effective. How would your body function if your hand decided to ignore orders from the brain and act on its own? Or your feet or eyes or mouth? (Sometimes my mouth seems to do just that!) What if your two hands had such differences they could not work together, and one tried to take your shirt off while the other tried to put it on? Or what if a hand got cross with your mouth and began punching it out? The body works only because its members are subject to the head. Caspian's council worked only because the diverse animals subjected themselves to his authority. The church works only when all its members subject themselves to its authority, which is Christ himself.

When we all submit to the same authority, we all have the same goal and cooperate together, support and assist, hurt with, and love one another. We are committed to one another because we are committed to the Head. As the apostle John wrote, "If we walk in the light as He is in the light, we have fellowship with one another."[14] When we are committed to the Head, we journey together toward a common goal, which is ultimate union with Christ.

IS THE CHURCH REALLY NECESSARY?

If at times you find yourself unenthusiastic about attending your church; if the choir is a little flat, the members a little self-absorbed, the classes a little dreary, the preaching a little, well, boring, you may be tempted just to skip church and spend the day at the lake. That temptation is not uncommon. No doubt you've encountered many Christians who see the church as a stuffy place filled with hypocrites, and they can worship God just as well out by themselves among the wonders of nature.

But before you pull away from the church, think about this: Where would the church be if everyone took that attitude? It would disappear. And then where would our declining society find the stabilizing influence the church brings in holding the line on truth and moral issues? If the corporate church disappeared, where would hurting people turn in times of trouble, as they do in droves to churches? If the church disappeared, what would happen to the hospitals, charitable foundations, homeless shelters, food banks, crisis centers, shelters for unwed mothers and battered women, programs for the addicted, and orphans' homes that churches fund and maintain all over the nation? None of this would be possible if on Sunday mornings we all slapped off our alarms, rolled over, and went back to sleep. Without our attendance and support, there would be no church to man and fund these functions.

And how could Christians maintain the courage, focus, and mutual support we've discussed in this chapter without a church that meets regularly? You need the church, and the church needs you. As in Narnia, differences may sometimes keep us from enjoying one another momentarily, but those same differences properly directed by the Head become great assets to all, and we cut ourselves off from others at our own peril.

Lewis himself, as a new convert, disliked church and avoided it for a while. As he told it, "I thought that I could do it on my own, by retiring to my rooms and reading theology, and I wouldn't go to the churches and Gospel Halls; and then later I found that it was the only way of flying your flag." Gradually he realized the value of mixing with members of every economic and educational level and came to understand that these people had such devotion and love for the Lord that he was not worthy to clean their boots.[15]

Lewis learned to get off his high horse and quit supposing for himself a superiority that enabled him to "do it on his own." If we must stoop a little to enter the door of the church, so much the better. It gives us the humility we need to accept one another in mutual love and respect.

CHAPTER 13

THE BLIND DWARFS
Faith and Sight

They have chosen cunning instead of belief. Their prison is only in their own minds, yet they are in that prison; and so afraid of being taken in that they cannot be taken out.

—ASLAN, *THE LAST BATTLE*

———————

In the final Narnia book, *The Last Battle*, a great deception occurs that challenges the faith of all Narnians and throws the kingdom into fatal confusion. On the first page we are introduced to a devious ape, Shift, who devises a plan to take over Narnia. He manipulates a not-too-clever donkey into wearing a lion skin and posing as Aslan. Speaking as the mouthpiece for the false Lion, Shift succeeds in duping and enslaving most of the Narnian creatures. He brings in the Calormenes as their taskmasters, who begin destroying the Narnian forests for timber. When Narnia's King Tirian exposes the false Aslan, he expects his kingdom to return to normal. But he realizes how mistaken he is when he rescues a group of black dwarfs who are being marched off into Calormene slavery. Instead of resuming their trust in Aslan, the dwarfs refuse to believe in the Lion any longer. As the dwarf Griffle explains, "We've been fooled once and we're not going to be fooled again." To Tirian's claim that Aslan is real, the dwarfs reply, "Where's he? Who's he? Show him to us!"

Things do not get better. The confusion over who Aslan really is undermines the faith of the Narnians until Tirian, Eustace, Jill, a dwarf, and a unicorn are the only remaining true believers. The Calormene army attacks the tiny company and throws them, along with the skeptical dwarfs, into a dark stable to be killed. These true Narnians, to their great surprise, find themselves not inside a stable but in a beautiful, sunlit land. The dwarfs, on the other hand, are convinced that they are imprisoned in the dark shed. Though Tirian and the children offer several proofs to the contrary, the dwarfs explain away each of them. Even when Aslan comes and provides a feast of pies, pigeons, trifles, ices, and wine in golden goblets, the dwarfs believe they are eating only the kinds of things one would find in a stable—hay, an old turnip, raw cabbage, and dirty drinking water.[1]

These dwarfs live in the hell they have created in their own minds. They will believe only what they can see, but they will see only what they believe. Evidence has no effect because they interpret all proofs in the light of what they have chosen to believe.

The dwarf mind-set is alive and well in our world. Many unbelievers live in self-imposed darkness, seeing life as a meaningless, dead-end journey filled with pain and tragedy. They taste only bad turnips and dirty water. Evidence attesting to the light of God shining through the clouds assails them from all sides, but they close their eyes to it. As Lewis tells us elsewhere: "The conflict is not between faith and reason, but between faith and sight."[2]

Everyone Exercises Faith

C. S. Lewis had the utmost respect for the intelligence and integrity of many unbelievers, but he was convinced that they committed errors of logic or allowed deep-rooted biases to keep them from seeing that Christianity is true. Their basic error was in following the lead of modern science and demanding empirical data to confirm all beliefs. Some truths, however, cannot be verified empirically, and

Christianity is one of these. Therefore unbelievers dismiss it as a blind faith that believers hold to without evidence.

Lewis wrote two essays defending Christianity against this charge.[3] In one he explains that different types of knowledge require different kinds of proofs. "The mathematician's proof . . . is by reasoning . . . the historian's by documents, the judge's by concurring sworn testimony."[4] The last two of these proofs, at least, require the exercise of faith, and it's a kind of faith that everyone—including the most rational scientist and the most logical mathematician—depends on daily. We believe that William the Conqueror invaded England, not because we have empirical proof (we weren't there), but because of documents recording the event that we judge to be reliable. Though I have never seen the Grand Canyon, I believe it has color and grandeur far beyond what the photos show, because several trustworthy witnesses have told me so.

Even the most materialistic scientist holds beliefs based on this kind of evidence. He buys a house believing the deed to be valid, because he trusts the title company's documents. He doesn't stop to examine the beams and supports of every bridge he approaches; he drives across, confident that the bridge is reliable. In other words, he exercises faith. No one demands empirical proofs for all beliefs. Testimony, documents, and common sense justify belief in many things that we cannot and need not prove empirically. And such beliefs are not empty hopes or wishful thinking; we accept them utterly and rightly give them the status of truth.

THE STEP BEYOND REASON

Religious faith is this type of belief. While neither Christianity nor atheism is supported by empirical evidence, Christianity is strongly supported by multitudes of these other kinds of evidences—credible testimony, reliable documents, historical corroboration, archaeological finds, and reason. It is simply wrong to claim that Christians believe in spite of evidence. To the contrary, we believe *because* of evidence. Blind faith is neither required nor admired.

Although the Christian faith has a strong, rational base, the unbelieving dwarfs in *The Last Battle* demonstrate Lewis's contention that a conviction based solely on evidence is not enough. Another element must be added to our rational assent to truth, and that is *trust*. To illustrate, let's look at what happens when Lucy returns from her first solitary trip through the wardrobe. She excitedly tells the others of her adventure. They don't believe her, and when they go to the wardrobe to test her story, they find that it has a solid back with no hint of entry into an alternate world. But Lucy sticks to her story even in the face of her siblings' disbelief, leading them to wonder about her sanity. They take the matter to their host, Professor Kirke. The wise old professor points out several facts the children have ignored: Lucy has always been truthful and reliable. It is obvious that she is perfectly sane. In spite of the extraordinary nature of her claim, they have no proof that it could not happen. So until evidence to the contrary turns up, the only sensible course is to *trust* her and assume that she is telling the truth.

The professor's answer to the children resembles what is perhaps the most quoted of all Lewis passages, popularly known as the Lewis Trilemma, in which he points out the fallacy of accepting Jesus as a great moral teacher while rejecting his claim to be God:

> A man who was merely a man and said the sort of things Jesus said would not be a great moral teacher. He would either be a lunatic—on a level with the man who says he is a poached egg—or else he would be the Devil of Hell. You must make your choice. Either this man was, and is, the Son of God: or else a madman or something worse.[5]

Logic and reason are involved in Professor Kirke's belief in Lucy's story, just as they are involved in our belief that Jesus is God.

But, like the Pevensie children, we are asked to take one step beyond reason into trust and believe in a world we cannot see. No evidence can show Lucy's siblings that Narnia exists. Yet they can rationally believe it does because of their experience with the truthfulness and sanity of their sister. Scientifically verifiable evidence cannot prove that Jesus is the Son of God, but reason can affirm the claim because everything Jesus says and does shows that he is neither demonic nor insane. The only rational alternative is to believe that he is who he says he is. In other words, it is *reasonable* to believe.

Rational faith is something altogether different from blind faith. Rational faith is based first on reason and then on trust. The evidences for the supernatural claims of Christianity are so overpowering that it's reasonable to believe. Trust maintains our hold on what reason tells us is true. Believing on the basis of evidence is easy. Raising that belief to the level of trust often is not. Trust requires risk because it means you must place yourself in the hands of the one you trust.

A good example occurs in *Prince Caspian* when the four children and the dwarf Trumpkin try to find their way to Caspian's camp. They agree on a direction and plunge into the woods. Underbrush, tangles, and ravines foil them continually, and they become tired and snappish. That night Aslan appears to Lucy and shows her the right direction. But when she tells the others, they do not believe her and continue in their own way. The obstacles get worse, forcing them to retrace their steps. The Lion again appears to Lucy while the others are sleeping, and this time she determines to follow him regardless of what they do. She awakens them and tells them that Aslan is waiting to show the way. Though none of them can see the Lion, Edmund agrees to go with Lucy. "She's been right before," he explains. The others follow reluctantly.

Aslan leads Lucy toward a sheer cliff, and he appears to have plunged over it. When she reaches the edge, however, she sees him descending a path into the gorge, giving them a straight shot to

Caspian's camp. The others cry for her to come back from the danger, but Edmund assures them, "No, she's right. There *is* a way down."[6] Moments later Edmund sees a moving shadow—the shadow of Aslan—and when they reach the bottom, he sees the Lion fully and runs to him in joy.

Even before these events Edmund has believed in Aslan. He has had clear evidences of his care and sovereignty. But in a time of extreme difficulty, he, like the others, reverts to his own self-sufficiency. And when he does, the Lion becomes invisible to him. Edmund decides to believe Lucy's claim to see Aslan on the basis of her history of truthfulness. But he does more than just believe; he follows her even though he himself cannot see. Edmund does not merely *have* faith; he *exercises* faith. He trusts in what he cannot see, because he trusts another who can see. And Edmund's trust is rewarded. Soon he sees the Lion dimly; as he continues to follow, his vision improves until he can see him clearly. The reward of trust is an increase in confidence and certainty.

The way to improve one's faith is to exercise trust, as Edmund did. God demands trust of us, because often he must lead us in directions that seem to defy reason. It may appear that he is about to lead us over a cliff, but when we trust and follow, a path opens up. Lewis explains that God demands such trust of us because at times the only way to help is to do the opposite of what seems helpful. We can understand this when we try to help others. "We are asking them to trust us in the face of their senses, their imagination, and their intelligence. We ask them to believe that what is painful will relieve their pain and that what looks dangerous is their only safety."[7] To release a dog's leg from a trap, it may be necessary to first move it further into the trap. Extracting a thorn from a child's finger may require cutting a little way into the skin to reach it. To teach a child to swim, one must convince him that permeable water will support him. Trust is necessary, because sometimes the only way to achieve results is to perform in ways that defy appearances.

From Propositions to a Person

Christian faith not only puts us on the right path, as in the Narnian examples above; it also brings us into a relationship with a person. Aligning our minds with the facts and accepting Christianity as true is an excellent first step, but that alone does not accomplish what God has in mind for us. He wants us to know him personally. He wants to restore the relationship that Adam and Eve lost in Eden, so you can know him face to face as the children in Narnia know Aslan. As Lewis puts it, "You are no longer faced with an argument which demands your assent, but with a person who demands your confidence."[8] God wants your confidence because he wants you.

No doubt you can see a problem here. An evil person or a con man would make the same demands as God does. And to put that kind of trust in such a person, as followers of cult leaders have done, can be fatal. How can you know your plunge of faith is justified? The key is to remember that blind faith is never required. Before you jump, be sure there is water in the pool. Explore the rational underpinnings of Christianity until you are sure they are solid and reliable. Let your mind be convinced that your faith is reasonable and that the claims of Jesus are not those of a con man. Even after you have done all this, the fact remains that a leap of faith is required as you follow the direction in which reason points and step onto the invisible path. Ultimately you have to follow your belief and trust. Make the plunge. You can't learn to ride a bicycle without getting on one. You can't learn to swim without jumping in the water.

In George MacDonald's story *The Golden Key*, the path of the girl Tangle leads to a great hole in the ground. "That is the way," her guide tells her. "But there are no stairs," she replies. "You must throw yourself in," he answers. "There is no other way."[9] Believing that Jesus is who he says he is will set you on the path, but it will lead you to a place where you cannot continue unless you throw yourself in.

Once we are rationally convinced that Christianity is true,

arguments against it will seldom sway us. But when we are called to put our convictions on the line, to go it alone when others urge us in their direction, to sacrifice financial security for a conviction, or when our own inner demons of lust, fear, jealousy, or greed tug at us to get off the narrow path—that's when faith is tested. That's when assent to a set of facts is not enough. That's when we need a real relationship with a real person we can trust.

Once that relationship is established and tested a few times, we will develop the confidence to do anything God asks. In *The Magician's Nephew* Aslan sends Digory Kirke on that journey into the Western Wild, far over the distant peaks to a valley walled by mountains of ice. Digory agrees to take on the daunting task even before he has any idea of how he can accomplish it.[10] He already believes in the Lion, and his experience with him results in a relationship, which gives him confidence that he can do whatever Aslan asks him to do.

The Bible is filled with people whom God asked to do seemingly impossible tasks. He asked Moses to lead a few million slaves out of the most powerful nation on earth. He asked Gideon to defeat a massive Midianite army with only three hundred men. He asked Mary to bear his own Son, becoming pregnant before she was wed, sacrificing her reputation, and enduring the gossip of the town. In each case the answer was the same as Digory's. The difficulty was not a factor. These men and women would do whatever God asked.

But What If I Am Wrong?

Today we often hear the claim that all religions are essentially the same and that we all really serve the same God. This is emphatically not the case. The pantheistic, nonpersonal god of the Hindus and Buddhists is a concept altogether different from the personal God of the Christians. The Allah of Islam has a far different personality and requires radically different responses from his adherents than the God of Christianity. My purpose in this chapter is not to present arguments defending Christianity as the one true religion. But I want to raise the question: What if we honestly make the wrong choice and put our faith in a false god?

In Narnia we find the answer in the soldier Emeth, the honest Calormene in *The Last Battle*. Emeth is a young officer in the army that invades Narnia. All his life he has served the Calormene god Tash, believing with all his heart that Tash is good and Aslan evil. When Emeth sees his leaders use treachery to deceive the Narnians and mock the god Tash by combining his name with Aslan's, the young man is deeply disturbed. He hates lies and trickery, and he loves truth and goodwill, attributes he believes reside in Tash. So when the ape says that Tash is in the dark stable (where the Calormene leaders have rigged a death trap for Narnians), Emeth insists on going inside. He is warned of the danger, but he replies, "Gladly would I die a thousand deaths if I might look once on the face of Tash."[11] He enters and disappears.

Immediately Emeth finds himself in a glorious country (the Narnian heaven), where he meets the great Lion Aslan—the most beautiful sight he has ever seen. He falls at his feet, ready to die for having served the wrong god. But to his great surprise, the Lion kisses him and says, "Son, thou art welcome." Emeth does not understand, and Aslan explains: "Child, all the service thou hast done to Tash, I account as service done to me." The confused young man asks if this means that Aslan and Tash are truly the same. The Lion growls until the earth shakes, not in anger but because the idea is utterly false. He explains that it is because he and Tash are opposites that he accepts the service that Emeth has rendered to Tash. No service that is vile can be done to Aslan, and no service that is good can be done to Tash. If any person does a kindness in the name of Tash, it is Aslan whom he really serves, and Aslan will reward him. But if one does a cruelty in Aslan's name, it is Tash whom he really serves.[12]

Emeth sought good, though under the wrong name, and by the Author of all good, he is accepted and rewarded. The truth is not in the name, but in the reality behind the name. The truth that Emeth loves is true truth, though he has mislabeled it. And Aslan accepts him because of his diligent dedication to what Aslan really is.

Aslan's acceptance of Emeth follows the principle Jesus taught when he explained how he will judge us when he comes again. He will separate everyone either on his right hand or his left. He will invite those on his right into his kingdom because they fed him when he was hungry, showed hospitality when he was a stranger, clothed him when he lacked clothing, and ministered to him when he was sick and in prison. Those on the right will be surprised to hear this. "When did we do all these things?" they will ask. Jesus will answer that every time they did good things for anyone, they did them for Jesus.[13] Like Emeth, those who dedicate themselves to meeting needs and following truth may not be conscious that they are doing these things as to Jesus, but Jesus accepts them in that way.

The apostle Paul tells us that this principle applies even when those who follow the law of God have no way of knowing it to be his law: "Even when Gentiles, who do not have God's written law, instinctively follow what the law says, they show that in their hearts they know right from wrong. They demonstrate that God's law is written within them, for their own consciences either accuse them or tell them they are doing what is right."[14]

Our faith justifies us, not on the basis of parroting the right words, or even on the basis of appending the right name to God, but rather on our commitment to conform ourselves to his true character. Those who desire goodness really desire the one, true God from whom all goodness flows. As the Lion told Emeth, whom he called "Beloved," "unless thy desire had been for me thou wouldst not have sought so long and so truly. For all find what they truly seek."[15]

Here Aslan accurately reflects the words of Jesus in the Sermon on the Mount: "Ask, and it will be given to you; seek, and you will find; knock, and it will be opened to you."[16] If you are honestly seeking God, you need not worry about finding him. He will find you.

PART 3

THE END
AND THE
BEGINNING

CHAPTER 14

BEYOND THE SHADOWLANDS

The Supernatural Parallel World

But do you really mean, Sir, that there could be other worlds—
all over the place, just around the corner—like that?
—PETER, THE LION, THE WITCH AND THE WARDROBE

———◆———

Have you ever seen a ghost? An angel? Or heard a voice speaking when you were certain no one was there? I've had none of these experiences, but I know people who say they have. Some of these reports, I admit, I seriously doubt. But I dare not dismiss all of them out of hand, because we have good reason to believe that there is an invisible spirit world alongside our visible one; it's beyond my range of knowledge to claim that the barrier between them is inviolable. In fact, I think there's more reason to believe that it is not.

PARALLEL WORLDS

The Narnia stories reflect Lewis's conviction that a world parallel to ours and invisible to us does exist. He shows the Narnian world to be solid and physical, like ours. Existing parallel and invisible to Narnia is a supernatural realm in which the Emperor-beyond-the-Sea resides and from which Aslan comes. Doors and portals open and close between Narnia and this supernatural realm, and many of the characters, both good and evil, enter and leave, voluntarily or otherwise.

We find an account of entry into this parallel world in *The Silver Chair* when Eustace and Jill, running from school bullies, escape through an ordinary door and find themselves in a place that we later learn is Aslan's country—a place not in Narnia but existing in a realm above it. In *The Last Battle* we learn that Aslan's country is within the Narnian heaven, a reality existing simultaneously with Narnia but not visible to it. This is Narnia's supernatural realm, what we would call the spirit world.

In placing a supernatural dimension above Narnia, Lewis follows the lead of the apostle Paul, who more than once refers to beings living in "the unseen world" that exists above our visible one. (Some Bible translations use the phrase "heavenly realms." The phrase does not refer necessarily to the heaven that Christians anticipate as their eternal home. It simply means the invisible world of spirits.) Paul tells us that our battle with evil is not against flesh and blood, but against "the evil rulers and authorities of the unseen world."[1] This world is invisible to us, but it's not because it contains nothing material to see. Angels exist as solidly and materially as we do, but they are inaccessible to our senses because they live in this unseen parallel world—what we might call another dimension.

REALITY AND SHADOWLANDS

To understand Narnia fully we must get inside C. S. Lewis's mind and understand how he structured its two dimensions—the natural and the supernatural—to relate to each other. We find the key in Plato. Lewis certainly did not subscribe to everything Plato postulated about the supernatural, but he believed his conception of archetypes meshes well with Christian theology. Plato's famous illustration of shadows in a cave explains his idea that everything in the material world is a lesser image of an ideal perfection that exists in a supernatural dimension. The illustration is fairly complex, but I will simplify it here to focus on those elements that illumine Lewis's thinking.

Imagine a person sitting with his back to the opening of a cave. The only light comes into the cave from behind him. He has always been chained so that he cannot turn his head toward the light, and all he has ever seen are dark shapes moving on the back wall of the cave. These shapes are actually shadows of real people passing behind the seated figure but in front of the light. The sitting person, with no other experience to guide him, sees these shadows as the true and only reality. If he manages to escape his chains and wander out of the cave, the bright light will blind him and cause him to think he is in a less substantial world than his dark cave. The real figures that cast the shadows will be so flooded with light that they will seem ghostly to his eyes, which are too acclimatized to darkness to see them clearly. The appearance will be the opposite of the facts.

Lewis saw in Plato's illustration a truth about nature and supernature and our perception of both. The supernatural—the world outside the cave—is the ultimate reality, and all things in nature are lesser copies or shadows of it. This is why once or twice Aslan refers to Narnia as the *Shadowlands*, a term which Lewis himself used to refer to our own world (and which gave the title to a stage play and two motion pictures on the marriage of Lewis to Joy Davidman).

Lewis follows the Platonic concept in his Narnian heaven, presenting it, not as a sterile state of ethereal wispiness, but as a reality more beautiful and substantial than the Narnia below it. His imaginative picture of heaven in *The Great Divorce* helps to explain the difference between the heavenly and earthly Narnias, and thus the difference between our own material world and the spirit world above it. In *The Great Divorce* tourists from a limbolike place journey to the edge of heaven. They begin as ordinary people with ordinary bodies but find themselves appearing wispy and wraithlike when they arrive in heaven. Everything there is more real than they are. The grass is too hard and unbending to walk on, and drops splashing from a waterfall could pierce them like bullets. But the long-term citizens of heaven, who are solid, beautiful, majestic, and glowing with extraordinary health, can splash in the water and walk through the grass with ease—which to their feet is soft and fresh.

The parallel to our world is clear. This present world is the Shadowlands. The supernatural world is the true reality. If spirits are invisible to us, it is because they are too solid for our senses. If the resurrected body of Jesus was able to pass through walls, it was not because his body was less substantial than the wall, but because it was more substantial, and the wall could not prevent it. All of Narnia is constructed on this principle that the supernatural is the solid reality and the natural is the shadow.

THE RATIONAL STEAMROLLER

Belief in the supernatural has always been part of humanity's make-up. Gods, goddesses, demons, spirits, sacrifice, and worship fill the pages of history in all cultures over the entire world. Prehistoric artifacts indicate the worship of nature and animals. The ancient Egyptians, the Mesopotamian cultures, the Mediterranean empires, and European civilizations all had their deities and religions. The same is true of the tribes in Africa, the Incas of South America, the native Indians in Central and North America, and the nations of the Orient. Although many of these cultures no doubt had those within them who questioned these supernatural gods, as did some Greeks of Paul's time, widespread belief in the supernatural remained essentially unchallenged until modern times.

In the eighteenth century Enlightenment philosophers began to insist that reason should affirm everything we know. The scientific age built on this foundation of rationalism and added a demand for empirical proof for all beliefs: I will believe only what I can see, hear, or touch. And the successes of science have affected society so widely that the materialistic outlook held by most scientists has come to dominate Western culture. Scientific theories proposing natural origins of the universe coupled with extreme rationalism have pushed supernatural beliefs to the sidelines. According to modern thought, the supernatural is a superstition, heaven is wishful thinking, spirits are fantasies, miracles could never happen, Christ was merely a man, and God does not exist. So many have bought into these assertions that religious belief is under fire and Christianity is on the defensive.

After his conversion to Christianity in 1931, the highly rational C. S. Lewis became an out-and-out supernaturalist. But he did not abandon his firm commitment to logic and rational thinking. Lewis's superbly reasoned defenses of the supernatural and the existence of God led author Chad Walsh to dub him "the apostle to the skeptics." But in Narnia Lewis bypasses rational argument and presents the supernatural in story as the only viable alternative to the dreary and meaningless material world that the materialists insist is the only reality.

Puddleglum, the marsh-wiggle in *The Silver Chair*, along with the human children Eustace and Jill, must descend deep into the Underland to free a Narnian prince from an evil enchantment. They have just accomplished their task and are about to escape when the evil queen enters. She throws a hypnotic powder on the fire and begins strumming an instrument to lull her foes into a stupor. As their minds grow foggy, she tells them there is no Narnia. They have merely imagined that bright world of color and beauty out of their own longings. She questions them about their Narnia, and Puddleglum and the children try to describe it. They tell her of the sun and of Aslan; when she asks them to describe these things, they compare them to a lamp and a cat, though much brighter and more glorious. The witch debunks their claims:

You have seen lamps, and so you imagined a bigger and better lamp and called it the *sun*. You've seen cats, and now you want

a bigger and better cat, and it's to be called a lion. Well, 'tis a
pretty make-believe, though, to say truth, it would suit you all
better if you were younger.[2]

Soon they succumb to the witch's enchantment and admit that
there is no Narnia.

The rational mind-set of today has "enchanted" many into believing that everything in the supernatural world is made up of bigger
and better imaginary images drawn from our own experiences. Just
as the witch tells Puddleglum and the children they are too old for
such play tales, today's rationalists tell us we are naive to believe in
the supernatural. They think that their feet are firmly planted on
hard reality and that in rejecting the supernatural they reject a fantasy. They do not realize they are under the enchantment of the
witch of rationalism.

There is too much that rationalism cannot explain for us to
dismiss the supernatural out of hand. One of these is the fact of
existence itself. There is no rational, scientific, or natural explanation for the existence of things. Either matter and energy existed
always, a theory that defies reason and nature; or it came into existence on its own, which defies reason and nature; or it was created
by a self-existent being, which also defies reason and nature. No natural explanation is possible. The simple fact of existence forces us to
admit the supernatural.

We may be drawn toward the supernatural because we are partly
supernatural ourselves. As Lewis says in *The Four Loves*, "We are
composite creatures, rational animals, akin on one side to the angels,
on the other to tom-cats."[3]

NOT ALL THAT'S SPIRITUAL IS GOOD

In *Prince Caspian* the dwarf Nikabrik does not believe in Aslan or
the ancient stories of the four Pevensies who ruled Narnia in its

golden days. He does not believe they can be called back in times of extreme need. But he does believe in the dark powers of hags, were-wolves, and the ancient White Witch. When Caspian's followers become desperate, Nikabrik proposes to enlist these evil beings to help them conquer King Miraz.

Though it may seem strange that people would reject the supernatural God then turn to supernatural occult powers, they may have reasons deeper than they can understand themselves. Materialistic philosophy simply does not meet our deep-seated need for transcendence. Materialism is like the false front of a movie set. It looks like a true reality, but it is merely an empty shell. Everyone who is not conditioned otherwise, and even many who are, looks for meaning outside the material world. Often people who suppress belief in God turn to mediums and spiritualism to find a transcendental connection that materialism denies them. When these people call on spirits, they may get more than they bar-gain for because the spiritual world is not inherently good but con-sists of both good and evil beings.

So why does Nikabrik turn to the dark powers instead of Aslan? He gives us the answer. He needs the power and the help that super-natural beings will give him, but he does not want to submit to Aslan's rules. His attitude may explain why people reject God yet turn to the occult in our world. In turning to God we are required to give up our selves and submit to his will. But the occult powers can be bargained with and manipulated for our own purposes. "We want a power that will be on our side," says Nikabrik.[4] He points out that the White Witch is such a power. She once executed the Lion, ruled Narnia for one hundred years, and imposed winter on the land. He will align with any power that will accomplish his ends, even if it destroys all that is valuable. Like Nikabrik, humans will inevitably connect to some supernatural power, either purposely or unwittingly, and any power other than the loving and creative God above the uni-verse will bring destruction.

Even people who do not believe in spirits, yet dabble in spirituality as a game or for other purposes, may get more than they bargain for. This principle is chillingly illustrated in *The Last Battle* when the Calormene conspirators taking over Narnia call on the false god Tash, whom they do not believe in, in order to deceive the gullible Narnian creatures. To their fatal dismay, a real evil spirit comes to them. "People shouldn't call for demons unless they really mean what they say," observes the dwarf Poggin.[5]

THE SUPERNATURAL AND YOU

Narnia affirms the supernatural by taking it for granted. It is not proposed or defended as a philosophic view of reality; it is just there, woven into the fabric of the stories so thoroughly that it can't be extricated from it. Lewis is telling us to accept the supernatural behind our own world in the same way. This supernatural realm is where God resides. He is the grand truth above all things that shines through the natural world like sunlight through clouds. It is an obvious fact if we don't close our eyes to the evidences of reason and deny the instinctive pull toward God that resides in our own makeup.

So what does this supernatural world mean to you in practical terms? Why should you care? You should care because what happens in the supernatural realm affects you deeply. The inhabitants of Narnia must deal with evil in the material world that began in the invisible world outside their own. So must we. Paul tells us of a battle raging in the spiritual realm. "For we are not fighting against people made of flesh and blood, but against the evil rulers and authorities of the unseen world, against those mighty powers of darkness who rule this world, and against wicked spirits in the heavenly realms."[6] This warfare raging around us in the invisible supernatural realm is for our very souls.

This realization moved actor-director Mel Gibson to say in an interview, "Somehow we humans are a lot more important in the cosmic scheme of things than we ever imagined." We are the prizes in that war. Which of these supernatural powers you align with determines your eternal destiny. The unbelieving dwarfs sit on the sidelines of the last battle, refusing to fight for either side. They are practical, businesslike, no-nonsense materialists, refusing to believe, refusing to commit, refusing to risk. As a result they miss out on the bountiful feast and beautiful land Aslan offers them. We must risk believing what we cannot see and choose sides.

Every act you perform shows which side you choose. Every act affects not only the future of this material world but extends into that invisible supernatural reality we call eternity. Begetting children and raising them to be Christians not only populates the earth but heaven as well. Giving a cup of cold water to a thirsty person earns an eternal reward. Those who do well with what they are given here will be rewarded with even greater gifts in the next world. How we love or hate others, how we do good or evil to them, can affect their own outlook on life and possibly determine whether they choose good or evil, heaven or hell. No deed we do is without consequences that extend past time and into eternity.

We are supernatural creatures ourselves, endowed with life that can extend past the material world as we know it and into eternity. We will do well to come to terms with the supernatural now and like Narnians learn to see its glimmer in all creation and begin to feel at home with it.

CHAPTER 15

FURTHER UP
AND FURTHER IN

A Glimpse into Heaven

The term is over: the holidays have begun.
The dream is ended: this is the morning.
—ASLAN, *THE LAST BATTLE*

Is the human mind really capable of imagining heaven? C. S. Lewis doubted it. Yet images of heaven fill many of his books, and as one writer said, "Lewis's imaginative realizations of heaven are the best and most convincing to appear in English literature since John Milton's *Paradise Lost.*"[1] No doubt the most striking and vivid of these appear in *The Last Battle*.

In this story the last Narnian king, Tirian, and a small company including Eustace, Jill, Jewel the unicorn, and Poggin the dwarf make a desperate last stand against an onslaught of Calormene soldiers. These valiant Narnians are greatly outnumbered, and the enemy forces them into the dark stable to be fed to their devouring god Tash. But once inside the stable, they are stunned to find themselves dressed in regal splendor and standing on rich, green grass among lovely fruit trees under a bright blue sky. Five royal-looking people stand nearby as if awaiting them. The five introduce themselves as Peter, Edmund, Lucy, Polly, and Digory, names that Tirian recognizes from Narnian history.

Peter explains how they got there. They were on a train in England, which seemed headed for a terrible wreck. They heard a roar and felt a lurch and immediately found themselves in this beautiful land, facing a door standing alone with no walls about it. They watched as several people and creatures came through the door including, finally, Tirian and his friends.

Soon after Peter's explanation, Aslan appears. He leads them to look through the door into the darkness that covers Narnia. Aslan calls for Father Time, and an enormous manlike shape looms on the dark horizon. As all watch, the stars begin to fall until the entire sky is empty and black. Streams of Narnian creatures leave the country and march through the door, where Aslan divides them to his right and left. Huge dragons and lizards appear in Narnia and consume all the foliage until nothing is left but bare rock and earth. The monsters shrivel and die, littering the wasteland with their bones. With a great roar, enormous waves of water roll in and bury the land. The dying sun consumes the moon, after which the hand of the giant Time squeezes it dark. The world freezes over, and Aslan tells King Peter to shut the door against the cold. Then the Lion bounds away, calling over his shoulder, "Come further in! Come further up!"[2]

No one can keep pace with Aslan, but they begin walking, greatly saddened by what they have just witnessed. Lucy cries. Digory regrets he has lived to see Narnia die. Jill says she had hoped Narnia would go on forever and thought it would. Tirian mourns the only world he has ever known.

THE LOSS OF OUR WORLD

We can understand these Narnians' grief over the loss of their world. Many of us feel the same way about the prospect of losing our own. We love the earth. I don't mean we love it in the way the apostle John warned us against loving it.[3] He was warning of loving what

Satan has warped into temptations to lure us from God. It is right that we love all the beauty and wonder of the earth that God created to be our home, but we will leave it someday. We know it shouldn't matter because heaven awaits us, yet like these Narnians, it saddens us to think about leaving all the joys we have known here. Frankly, I don't think many of us really anticipate heaven. Of course we say we do, but I don't detect much enthusiasm over the idea of going.

Mark Twain made an insightful observation that may explain our lack of enthusiasm for heaven. He noted that heaven seemingly contains little of what men and women enjoy most on earth, and it is filled with things they care little for. All sensual pleasure is absent, replaced with worship, praise, singing, making music, and a mix of people from all nations. Twain observed that few sing well on earth and spend little time trying. Few enjoy church attendance, even fewer have any interest in playing a musical instrument, and most people distrust members of other races. As Twain saw it, man's per-ception of heaven is a strange thing: "It has not a single feature in it that he actually values. It consists—utterly and entirely—of diver-sions which he cares next to nothing about, here in the earth, yet is quite sure he will like in heaven."[4]

This bitter agnostic was ridiculing us Christians, but he did make a valid point. If we were honest, most of us would admit that the heaven we imagine is not all that appealing. We enjoy our flesh-and-blood bodies (especially while young and healthy), yet most of us think that our heavenly bodies will be less than substantial and lacking desires and pleasurable sensations. We enjoy being active on earth. We throw ourselves into thousands of rewarding pursuits—building, man-agement, gardening, art, travel, sports—you name it. But we look toward a heaven of rest where we will have little or nothing to do. We love the mountains, streams, waterfalls, forests, and seashores of our earth, but we look toward a heaven of gold, crystal, and jewels—all metal, glass, and stones—the elements of urban settings we try to escape from on weekends.

We tend to think of heaven either as something like an elaborate retirement center or, from the description of the New Jerusalem in Revelation 21 and 22, as an architectural showplace designed as God's capital city. Most people dread living in retirement centers. As for capital cities, I stand in awe of the magnificent architecture and monuments of Washington, D.C. But as much as I appreciate the Lincoln Memorial, it's not my idea of a cozy home.

So what is wrong with this picture? Will heaven be a big let-down—a place where we are bored to tears, longing for the earth we knew? Or is it possible that we have a skewed picture of it? According to what Narnia shows us, the latter is the case. Our ideas about heaven miss the truth by light-years.

THE NEW NARNIA

After witnessing the death of Narnia, the little group turns westward to follow Aslan "further up and further in." They have no idea where they are, but they love what they see. "I bet there isn't a country like this anywhere in *our* world," says Eustace. "Look at the colors! You couldn't get a blue like the blue on those mountains in our world." Soon they sense something familiar about this beautiful land. Lucy notes that the woody hills ahead and the blue ones beyond look much like the southern border of Narnia.

> "Like!" cried Edmund after a moment's silence. "Why, they're exactly like. Look, there's Mount Pire with his forked head, and there's the pass into Archenland and everything!"
>
> "And yet they're not like," said Lucy. "They're different. They have more colors on them and they look further away than I remembered and they're more . . . more . . . oh, I don't know . . ."
>
> "More like the real thing," said the Lord Digory softly.

They are in a country exactly like Narnia, but brighter and more alive. As all this sinks in, Farsight the eagle flies into the air, soars around, and reports back to the group. "I have seen it all—Ettinsmuir, Beaversdam, the Great River, and Cair Paravel still shining on the edge of the Eastern Sea. Narnia is not dead. This is Narnia." The awed group continues westward, and they see more evidence that the eagle's words are true. Everything is Narnia, but "every rock and flower and blade of grass looked as if it meant more."[5]

As they journey, they notice the same kinds of differences in themselves that they have seen in this new Narnia. They are enhanced. They can run all day—even up steep slopes and through winding valleys—and never tire. They can plunge into icy water heedless of the cold or skim across lakes like speedboats. They even climb up a waterfall, a feat that would have drowned or smashed them to pieces in the old Narnia.

They ascend a hill topped by a walled garden, where they meet many Narnians from the past. The garden opens upon enormous vistas of hundreds of miles, which in that air they can see in great detail. As they gaze, it dawns on them that they are looking on England—not the old England but a new England glowing with the same kind of perfection, color, and vividness as the new Narnia.

Next they ascend a soaring, forested mountain. Near the top Aslan comes bounding to meet them. Lucy is afraid they will be sent away, but the Lion assures her, "No fear of that. Have you not guessed?" He explains that there really was a railway accident in England, and they are, as they called it in the Shadowlands, dead. Tirian and his little group also died when they were forced into the stable. But *dead* is an outrageous word for what they experience now. In Aslan's words, "The term is over: the holidays have begun. The dream is ended: this is the morning."[6] In the terms we use on earth, they have died and gone to heaven. But in reality they have come to their true home, and now they are truly alive for the first time. They are in the Narnian heaven.

OUT OF THE SHADOWLANDS

Early in this remarkable experience, Digory, who grew up to be Professor Kirke of *The Lion, the Witch and the Wardrobe*, figures out the meaning of the bright world they travel in. He tells the others that the old Narnia was not the true Narnia:

> It was only a shadow or a copy of the real Narnia. . . . All of the old Narnia that mattered, all the dear creatures, have been drawn into the real Narnia through the Door. And of course it is different; as different as a real thing is from a shadow or as waking life is from a dream. . . . It's all in Plato.[7]

The old Narnia had to be destroyed because evil had contaminated it. All the good of that Narnia was drawn into the new, as we saw when Aslan separated the good creatures from the evil and sent the evil ones away. The air of the new Narnia is no longer "thick" with the effects of evil. Now it is pure, clean, exhilarating air that does not impede any action or thought. The new Narnia is free of all evil.

Yes, it is "all in Plato," but it is also a thoroughly biblical concept. Though the Bible tells us that the heavens and the earth will be destroyed, it also speaks of "a new heaven and a new earth."[8] Now if we're all destined to go to heaven, what is the point of a new earth? Part of the answer lies in the erroneous idea suggested in the phrase *go to heaven.* In the book of Revelation we read of "the holy city, New Jerusalem, coming down out of heaven."[9] The description of this city gives us the picture of heaven that permeates popular imagination— the high golden walls with twelve gates of pearl, the streets of transparent gold, the crystal-clear waters, and the throne of God. Revelation is a complex and puzzling book; but we can be sure that whether this golden city is literal or figurative, it conveys to us a real truth.

Notice two things about the city: First, it comes down *from heaven to earth.* Second, after it descends, a loud voice booms from heaven saying, "Behold, the tabernacle of God is with men, and He will dwell with them, and they shall be His people. God Himself will be with them and be their God."[10] We have no indication here that we will go up to heaven, but rather the opposite; heaven will come down to us. If one takes this literally, it means the heavenly city will be nestled in the forests and waterfalls of earth. If we take it figuratively, it must mean that in some sense the Christian's future is one of God condescending to live with humans rather than drawing humans out of the environment made for them.

We see a further hint of what God is about when he says: "Behold, I make all things new."[11] Add this passage to the others, and we begin to see how the package wraps up. God will destroy the old earth as the Lion destroyed the old Narnia. And the reasons are the same. It's like burning away the old matted and diseased grass so a new lawn can grow. It's getting rid of the embedded disease of sin so that all things can blossom anew, fresh and pure. After destroying the old, God remakes the heavens and the earth. It's the restoration of all things as they were intended to be. And then, wonder of wonders, God himself comes down to live among us again just as he strolled the garden paths with Adam and Eve in the glowing twilight of Eden. The package is complete. Everything is to be put back just as God intended from the beginning. The whole idea of redemption is restoration. Our heaven will be a new Eden.

That is exactly the picture Lewis gives us in the new Narnia. Aslan destroys the old Narnia, but as the Narnians move deeper into the new land, they realize it is really the Narnia they have known all along but brighter, clearer, purer, more vivid, and more meaningful. They have not lost the Narnia they loved; it has been restored. And then, as they reach the mountaintop garden, who but Aslan comes bounding toward them. He assures the happy company that they will never be sent away from Narnia again. They will be with him in the new Narnia forever, just as God will come down and dwell with us.

Thus Narnia helps us adjust any false ideas we may hold about heaven. *The Last Battle* clarifies the picture, showing a heaven that is really a fresh new Narnia. Lewis's inclusion of England as part of the new lands shows that he means this picture to be more than a mere fantasy. Not only is the Narnia of his imagination to be restored, but also all that is good of the real earth.

WORLDS WITHOUT END

But, you may wonder, given the endlessness of eternity, no matter how grand and beautiful the earth and our bodies may be, after a few billion years, won't we eventually get bored? Narnia shows us the answer. With each cry of "further up and further in," the Narnians journey deeper into the new country and find new vistas opening continually before them, each larger and grander than the previous. The truth dawns on Lucy: "This is still Narnia, and more real and more beautiful than the Narnia down below, just as *it* was more real and more beautiful than the Narnia outside the stable door! I see . . . world within world, Narnia within Narnia."[12] The unfolding of the fresh and new will never end.

Gazing up into the nighttime sky, we often wonder why there are so many other worlds—why our planet is a pinpoint in relation to the uncountable galaxies out there. Narnia provides a clue. Could it be that all this is the yet unexplored territory where God will invite us to go "further up and further in"? The Bible tells us that we shall reign with Christ.[13] Though the nature of that reign is not described, we know we were created to be lords of the earth, subregents under God, carrying within us his Holy Spirit and acting as his deputies over creation. Maybe the universe is filled with new planets that God intends to develop. Maybe he wants us to be his coregents in these new worlds. It is easy to imagine that in eternity the role we were created for will still be ours, but expanded "further up and further in" forever reaching new worlds throughout the endlessness of space.

If we are to be God's representatives in worlds of new discovery without end, heaven will be anything but boring. Maybe that is the reason for the vastness of galaxy-filled space. It's got to match up with the endlessness of *forever*.

PARADISE RESTORED

We are told that we are already in the kingdom of God, and as Christians we can begin tasting the joys of heaven now.[14] This is how we prepare ourselves for our future. We learn to love heavenly things. This does not mean turning our backs on the physical and becoming "spiritual" in some unearthly sense that denies the world around us and concentrates on "higher" abstract values. It means that in this world we come to terms with what we will deal with in the next. If the next world is a perfect version of this one, that means we learn to care for what we've been given. We manage our present gifts efficiently; we care for the environment, do good to our neighbors, treat all creatures well, and enjoy the good but correct the bad. And in all this, we grow more fully aware of the Giver of all the good we experience and learn to love him with all our hearts.

These are the things we were created to do in the beginning, and except for correcting the bad effects of the Fall, they are what we will do on the new earth. We are in God's kingdom now. After death takes away the matted decay and mold of the Fall, we will still be in it, still charged with the same tasks but able to perform them with perfect bodies freed from contamination.

Shortly after the Narnians begin their journey into the new country, they enter a forest of incredibly beautiful trees loaded with fruit that looks too luscious to eat. They are hesitant to pluck the fruit, thinking a pleasure so tempting must be somehow wrong. But Peter tells them it's all right: "We've got to the country where everything is allowed."[15] In heaven all shame and guilt about experiencing pleasure will evaporate. Everything is allowed in heaven, just as everything was allowed on earth until sin twisted the use of things and lusts and addictions had to be taken into account. As the apostle Paul explained, "All things are lawful for me, but all things are not helpful. . . . I will not be brought under the power of any."[16] On earth our lusts and tendencies toward addiction put caution signs on pleasure. As Lewis expresses it elsewhere, we must wear clothes to protect ourselves from lust because we are fallen. But he adds, "The naked body should be there underneath the clothes, ripening for the day when we shall need them no longer."[17] In heaven we will find no boundaries on freedom, joy, delight, and ecstasy.

On their journey further up and in, the Narnians come across the donkey Puzzle, who had been manipulated by the evil ape. He is now an extraordinarily beautiful and graceful creature with a lustrous, silver gray coat and a gentle, honest face. "He was himself now."[18] The old Puzzle has become what he was intended to be all along. That is our future as well. When we put on those incorruptible bodies, we will then be what we were intended to be all along. Each of us will have extraordinary grace and beauty. All the corruptions to our genetic codes passed down by our ancestors will be corrected. Not only the major deformities, chronic illnesses, and irreparable damage, but also the little flaws—your mother's too-wide hips, Grandpa Wilson's weak chin, Uncle Hubert's bald spot, Aunt Judith's crooked teeth, and Grannie Smith's hooked nose. It will all be fixed. Like Puzzle we will be our intended selves. All of us will be "hotties"—cheesecakes and hunks.

If you still hold in your mind that picture of an insipid, sterile heaven that has constricted the imaginations of so many of us, let Narnia open your eyes. Like the new Narnia, heaven is filled with the joyful things we really love. It is our home. It's where we are meant to live. Heaven is the ultimate fulfillment of all the deepest desires you have right now. When Jewel the unicorn steps into that wonderful country, he exclaims:

I have come home at last! This is my real country! I belong here. This is the land I have been looking for all my life, though I never knew it till now. The reason why we loved the old Narnia is that it sometimes looked a little like this. . . . Come further up, come further in![19]

———•·•·•———

CHAPTER 16

LONGING FOR ASLAN
The Object of All Desire

*This was the very reason why you were brought to Narnia, that
by knowing me here for a little, you may know me better there.*
—ASLAN, THE LAST BATTLE

———◦◦◦———

Shasta, in *The Horse and His Boy*, often gazes toward the unknown
north, longing to know what lies beyond the village that is the only
home he knows. He sometimes asks his father, Arsheesh the
Calormene, about the north, but the fisherman tells him, "Do not
allow your mind to be distracted by idle questions."[1] When a
Tarkaan Lord comes to the hut to buy Shasta, the boy overhears
Arsheesh explain how he found Shasta as an infant in a boat washed
up on the shore. The revelation excites Shasta. It explains much.
He has never felt at home with Arsheesh, who has treated him not
as a son but a slave. Shasta is glad to know that he is native to
another country. Maybe he is from the north. He muses that he may
be anybody—even somebody. Perhaps even the son of a god.

Sooner or later virtually all of us feel the same kind of alien-
ation from our familiar world and an undefined longing for something beyond it. It may happen while gazing at a grand mountain
vista, holding a child in your arms, reading a great story, or listening
to a symphony. Or it may break in on you unexpectedly with no
apparent cause, as it first did on C. S. Lewis.

As a boy Lewis stood beside a flowering currant bush on a summer day. The memory of an exquisite toy garden his brother had made years earlier flooded him with a sensation he later described as "enormous bliss of Eden." He felt an overpowering desire, but a desire for what? He did not know. "Before I knew what I desired, the desire itself was gone, the whole glimpse withdrawn, the world turned commonplace again, or only stirred by a longing for a longing that had just ceased." The experience so overwhelmed Lewis that he said, "In a certain sense everything else that had ever happened to me was insignificant in comparison."² He used the German term *Sehnsucht* to identify this unidentified desire, which had a profound effect on everything he did and wrote for the rest of his life.

LOOKING FOR JOY IN ALL THE WRONG PLACES

Lewis learned by trial and error in his atheist years that the experience triggering the desire was not the satisfaction of it. The longing seemed to be for something he was meant to have but had not yet experienced. He did not yet identify the desire as hunger pangs originating in what Blaise Pascal called the "God-shaped vacuum" that exists in every human heart.

Although everyone feels this undefined longing, few recognize it for what it is. We can sense it in any beautiful thing—nature, art, literature, movies, music, or relationships. It is natural to think that the object triggering the desire should also fulfill it. But when we grasp for that thing to satisfy the longing, we find satisfaction to be as elusive as the rainbow. It evaporates and we come away empty. The longing may speak through nature and wear the lovely face of nature, but the true object of our desire lies beyond nature in a world that we cannot yet reach. If we realize the call comes not from these things themselves but from beyond them, we will find the true object of our longing.

You may first discover the longing on a forest trail and spend

your life traveling or camping, trying to find fulfillment in the perfect scenic view or in achieving oneness with nature. You may lock
in on family, career, friendship, romance, sex, food, drink, houses,
cars, books, movies, sports, or hobbies, therein seeking a satisfaction
you will never find, because the true object of your desire lies
beyond the experience that arouses it. We mistake the shadow for the
reality. We desire significance and try to achieve it by gaining a company title and a corner office. We desire security and try to find it in
sound investments, retirement funds, and paid-off mortgages. We
desire love and try to find it in ways good and bad—permanent relationships, temporary liaisons, friends, pets, organizations, fame, or
even church memberships.

But all these desires, whether satisfied poorly or well, are the diffused rays of a single desire that can be satisfied ultimately in only
one way: by a relationship with God. Only in him can we ever find
true significance, security, and love. Even the best of his gifts—the
most legitimate and rewarding of satisfactions on earth, such as a perfect marriage—can deflect us from finding him if we fail to follow
the desire through the gift to the Giver. This was the fatal problem
with the marriage of Sheldon and Davy Vanauken, mentioned in
chapter 11. Their love for each other excluded God. It cut them off
from the source of all love, which not only prevented their desire
from finding its ultimate fulfillment; it eventually would have with-
ered their love for each other. The greater the gift, the more it can
block the light of the Giver.

At the end of the *Chronicles*, we learn that Susan is not among
those entering the new Narnia, because her desires have distracted
her from Aslan. She desires to be "grown up." There's nothing wrong
with wanting to be mature and fulfilling one's potential, but Susan
has become distracted by the trappings of being grown up. "She's
interested in nothing nowadays except nylons and lipstick and invi-
tations," says Jill.[3] She has let the glitter of surface beauty deflect her
from the God whose love would endow her with more beauty and

maturity than she could ever dream of. We Narnia readers all hope that Susan comes to her senses, but as the Lion often says, "I tell no one any story but his own."

Edmund in *The Lion, the Witch and the Wardrobe* longs for significance. He may suffer from the "middle-child syndrome," perhaps feeling that Peter and Susan get all the privileges while the younger Lucy gets all the attention. He compensates by bullying and pestering Lucy. So when the White Witch offers him a throne in Narnia if he will betray his siblings, he jumps at the chance to rule over them. But all along Aslan has had a throne prepared for Edmund in Narnia; had he desired the Lion instead of the throne, the throne would have been freely given him (as indeed it is after the boy's repentance and Aslan's sacrifice). Satisfy your longings with substitutes, and you get only continuing emptiness. Satisfy them by loving God, and you get not only him but all his gifts as well.

How Can We Love God?

Even if we understand that God is the ultimate object of all desire—only he can fill that God-shaped vacuum—we still face a difficulty. How can we really *love* him in a meaningful way? The people we love in our world are with us in physical form. We can see them, talk with them, and hug them. Of course we know we can talk to God, and that he hears us. But we have no physical contact or audible feedback. He does not respond verbally or carry on a conversation as we do with our spouse or friend. So how can we really love him as we love friends and family?

Here is where Narnia helps us immensely. Like all good art, these seven stories illumine a truth and enable us to see it vividly—in some ways not merely to see it but to experience it. Narnia shows us the love of God so up close and personal that it's almost impossible not to respond. Aslan is to Narnians as Jesus is to us. He created a wonderful world for us. He loves us. He died for us. He works behind the scenes pulling the strings of providence. He responds to our prayers. He gives us joy. Aslan brings all that God does into sharp focus and makes it tangible and personal. This visible, touchable, and audible Lion loves his characters with endearing words, solicitous care, wise guidance, loving touches, and affectionate kisses. Aslan's bold contact with his creatures enables them to see and feel—no, it enables us to see and feel—exactly who it is that does all these things for us.

It's no wonder that nine-year-old Laurence, the boy we mentioned back in chapter 6, feared that he loved Aslan more than Jesus. Aslan opened his eyes to all the endearing qualities of Jesus that he had failed to see. He fell in love with Aslan, not realizing that for the first time, he was loving Jesus as he should.

Unlike the Narnians, who can see, hear, and touch Aslan, we no longer have Jesus in tangible form. But in these stories Lewis shows us the first step in learning to love Christ. We can see the boundless scope of his love in his gifts. That's why Narnia is filled with the delights of creation. Everything God made is for our delight and joy. In the *Chronicles* Lewis holds this truth up to our face so we can't possibly miss it. Rather than asking the tired old question, "Why is there so much evil in the world?" Narnia forces us to answer another question: "Why is there so much good in the world?" We can account for evil in the fact of our free will and the Fall. But if there is no God, how can we account for all the beauty, wonder, love, joy, and delight in the world?

The overwhelming good that shines through the Fall shows us not only a God who exists but a God of deep, rich, sacrificial, unending, joyful love. All creation is an act of love. The key to loving God as Laurence loved Aslan is to see God's love in every good thing that happens to us, both the large things and the small, to make that awareness the lens through which we view our existence. Every time you snuggle under a warm blanket on a cold night, know that God is loving you. Every time your daughter hugs you, be aware that she is passing on God's love. When the unexpected check arrives to cover the unplanned medical bill, or when you're turned down for the promotion then get a better offer from another company, know that God is pulling strings for you.

And you can use the same lens when things are not going so well. When your dear friend dies, know that God grieves with you, just as Aslan grieved over Digory's mother and Jesus wept at the tomb of Lazarus. Know that he is there; share your grief with him, and his Spirit within you will give you strength that you can know comes from him. This continual awareness of God's activity in your life is a kind of ongoing prayer that will draw you closer to him and increase your sense of his continual presence. Practice this and you will come to love Jesus as Laurence loved Aslan. And he will become as real to you as Aslan is to the Narnians. It will begin to dawn on you that Christ is the true object of all your longing.

Think about the greatest love you have ever known; it is only a dim shadow of the love that God has for you. When you finally see him, you will know that you have just met the love of your life. You will know that he is what you have really been dreaming of and longing for in every desire you ever had. When you see him, you will want nothing more than to spend all eternity basking in his presence.

REACHING ASLAN'S COUNTRY

When Reepicheep the mouse was in his cradle, a wood woman spoke a prophetic verse over him. He would find what he was seeking in the utter East where sky and water meet. "I do not know what it means," he tells Lucy. "But the spell of it has been on me all my life."[4] Reepicheep longs for Aslan's country, and his purpose in sailing on the *Dawn Treader* is to reach the utter East and fulfill this lifelong desire. The valiant mouse pursues his desire with single-minded determination:

While I can, I sail east in the *Dawn Treader*. When she fails me, I paddle east in my coracle. When she sinks, I shall swim east with my four paws. And when I can swim no longer, if I have not reached Aslan's country, or shot over the edge of the world in some vast cataract, I shall sink with my nose to the sunrise.[5]

After the ship enters a beautiful, still sea covered with silver white lilies, Reepicheep takes his little coracle and gets in a boat to head for the utter East. Edmund, Lucy, and Eustace, knowing it is time for them to return to their own world, go with him. They sail through the Silver Sea until they reach a giant, fixed wave beyond which a range of mountains rises so high they cannot see the tops of them. The boat runs aground, and Reepicheep paddles away in the coracle. The three children watch as he rows up the wave and disappears over the top. We know he reaches Aslan's country because we meet him there in *The Last Battle*.

The three children leave the grounded boat and wade southward, parallel to the wall of water. They reach dry land and begin walking across a vast plain of green grass. Soon they meet a pure white Lamb. When they tell the Lamb they are looking for Aslan's country, he changes into the golden Lion. Aslan tells the children they cannot come into his country yet but that there is a way into it from all worlds. Lucy is excited and asks him how one gets into his country from our world. "'I shall be telling you all the time,' said Aslan. 'But I will not tell you how long or short the way will be; only that it lies across a river. But do not fear that, for I am the great Bridge Builder.'"

As the Lion prepares to send the children into their world, Lucy asks when they can come back to Narnia—and she wants it to be soon. But Aslan tells her gently that she and her brother Edmund will never come back to Narnia. They must begin to grow up and learn to see the things of Narnia in their own world. His answer distresses Lucy, and it's not merely because she will never see Narnia again:

> "It isn't Narnia, you know," sobbed Lucy. "It's you. We shan't meet you there. And how can we live, never meeting you?"
>
> "But you shall meet me, dear one," said Aslan.
>
> "Are—are you there too, Sir?" said Edmund.
>
> "I am," said Aslan. "But there I have another name. You must learn to know me by that name. This was the very reason why you were brought to Narnia, that by knowing me here for a little, you may know me better there."[6]

Edmund and Lucy never return to the old Narnia, the shadow Narnia. But we learn in *The Last Battle* that they do reach the new and real Narnia and meet Aslan there. He explains to them that they have left the Shadowlands forever, and now they will live on in his presence, knowing his love face to face.

And then Lewis says, "As He spoke He no longer looked to them like a lion; but the things that began to happen after that were so great and beautiful that I cannot write them."[7]

If Aslan no longer looks like a Lion, it's not too hard to guess just what he does look like or who he is. Everything in Narnia leads ultimately to Aslan. Everything in our world leads ultimately to God. Everything in Narnia shouts the love of Aslan for his Narnians. Everything in our world shouts the love of God for us. Just as Narnia has Aslan, we have a God who loves us and desires nothing for us but ecstatic joy. Aslan is an accurate reflection of Jesus Christ. He calls us through every created thing to find in him the source of all joy and love him in return, thus finding our true selves in a relationship with the One whom we were created to love.

AFTERWORD

I hope you read the *Chronicles of Narnia* before you read this book. But I expect some readers did not. And I can understand. Perhaps they saw the movie or read one or two of the books, sensed the power and depth beneath the surface of the story, and wanted to explore the meaning of it. If this describes you, and you made it through this book in spite of having no prior experience with the *Chronicles*, I hope you will go back and read them now. I know I have spoiled many of the surprises and revealed the plots and essence of some of the stories. Surprise, however, is not the key to enjoying books like these. It's the flavor, the experience, the revisiting of places where you have been happy and found joy. You can go back to Narnia over and over, just as you can visit your favorite vacation spot or your favorite friends or relatives over and over and experience fresh enjoyment every time. It's like eating at a favorite restaurant to which you return many times, not because you look forward to the surprise of a new entrée, but because you like the ambiance and the menu.

When you read the *Chronicles*, I urge you not to try to remember the analyses and explanations I have given in this book. Just enjoy the stories. Forget the "lessons" and abandon any search for deeper meanings. The meanings in the stories will enter your soul through the stories themselves. You will *experience* the truths they contain instead of studying them and consciously applying them. The reading experience will nourish you, even if you aren't immediately aware of just what the stories are conveying, just as food nourishes you without your thinking about digestion.

From the *Chronicles of Narnia* you may wish to continue reading other C. S. Lewis fiction. He wrote four narrative novels: his science fiction trilogy, *Out of the Silent Planet*, *Perelandra*, and *That Hideous Strength*, and what many consider to be his best fiction, the mythic *Till We Have Faces*. Three other books, although not traditional novels, are fictional in nature: *The Screwtape Letters*, correspondence between a demon and his understudy on how to best tempt Christians, a blockbuster bestseller that got Lewis's picture on the cover of *Time* magazine, *The Great Divorce*, an excursion to the rim of heaven, and his allegoric, autobiographical *The Pilgrim's Regress*.

From there you may want to pursue his nonfiction. A good place to start is his ever-popular *Mere Christianity*; then perhaps *The Four Loves*; *Reflections on the Psalms*; *Letters to Malcolm, Chiefly on Prayer*; and books of essays such as *God in the Dock*, *The Weight of Glory*, *The World's Last Night*, and *Christian Reflections*. If you want to move on to his heavier works, you can try *Miracles*, *The Problem of Pain*, and *The Abolition of Man*. I call these "heavier" works because they deal with somewhat perplexing subjects and require a little more concentration than some of the others. But I think you will find that Lewis has a way of making complexity quite understandable. He, more than any author I know, is able to make clear and comprehensible concepts that I might find over my head when treated by other writers. I will not make any recommendations from his several volumes of literary analysis and criticism, though if you are interested in such, you have a real treat ahead of you.

I hope you will join me and the millions of other readers who have discovered the wealth of insight, truth, wisdom, creativity, and delight in reading the works of C. S. Lewis.

Discussion Questions

—◦•◦•◦—

Introduction

1. How did J. R. R. Tolkien use myth to convince C. S. Lewis that Christianity is true?
2. Does the term *myth* always mean untrue? What did Lewis mean by the phrase "myth became fact"?
3. What is the meaning of *escapism*? Is escapism good or bad?
4. What did Lewis mean when he said he hoped the Narnian stories would slip past the "watchful dragons" in readers' minds?
5. Do you agree that the "romantic" view of reality is the way we should see the world? Explain.
6. Explain the term *muggles*. Why is it so easy to become a muggle?
7. What is the connection of beauty, love, and joy to religion?

Chapter 1: Not a Tame Lion

1. Who is Aslan? What does it mean that he is the King?
2. What does Mr. Beaver mean when he says that Aslan is not safe, but he is good? How is it possible for Aslan to be, as C. S. Lewis describes him, both good and terrible?
3. Why do you think Lewis chose a lion instead of some other creature to be the Lord of Narnia?
4. Why won't God make us happy on our own terms?

5. What does it mean that "love is something more stern and splendid than mere kindness"? Why must love sometimes be severe?
6. Does God want us to be happy? Explain.
7. Why do some people find it hard to love God? How can reading about Aslan help overcome this difficulty?

CHAPTER 2: THE SONG OF ASLAN

1. Aslan sings Narnia into existence. Can you think of instances in the Bible where inanimate creation responds to the voice of Deity? Discuss the implications.
2. Narnia is still a place of beauty even after evil enters it. How can we learn to see the glory of original creation beneath all the corruption and ruin that now mars it?
3. What does it mean that humans are to fill the earth, subdue it, and have dominion over the living creatures?
4. How can reading fantasy reawaken our wonder at the beauty of creation?
5. Are our physical bodies evil? How are they important to who we are? Will we have physical bodies in heaven? Explain and discuss.
6. What is the difference between seeing the world through rose-tinted glasses and seeing it through polarized lenses?
7. What does creation show us about how we should see and treat one another?

CHAPTER 3: MAMMALS, MOUNTAINS, AND MUFFINS

1. Narnia is filled with simple, homey pleasures. What do everyday pleasures show us about God's love?
2. Narnia is also filled with grand, inspiring mountains and waterfalls. Why do grand vistas in nature, such as mountains and waterfalls, thrill and inspire us?

3. When a mountain or vista in nature evokes a longing in you, what is it that you long for?

4. Pleasure is presented unabashedly in Narnia. Should we freely enjoy pleasure or shun it as a temptation distracting us from spiritual matters? Explain.

5. Do our bodies, responding to pleasure, lead us into most of our sins? Explain.

6. Will the eventual destruction of the earth be permanent? Why or why not?

7. What is the underlying message we receive from the beauty and pleasure we experience in nature?

CHAPTER 4: BAD MAGIC

1. Digory seemingly could not resist striking the bell in Charn. Why do we feel a strong curiosity about the forbidden? Is this impulse good or bad? Why?

2. Why was the fact that Eve was deceived an inadequate excuse for disobeying God?

3. Given the great harm that Jadis the witch brought to Narnia, why did Aslan allow her presence there? Why did God allow Satan in Eden?

4. What was so terrible about Adam and Eve's simple act of disobedience? Why did this act result in the Fall?

5. Why does God allow the effects of Adam and Eve's sin to remain with us? Why doesn't he undo the damage and fix things back like he meant them to be?

6. Name and discuss some of the prominent characteristics of evil displayed in Narnia.

7. After the fall of mankind, did God rescind that great compliment of allowing us to be movers and shakers? Explain.

CHAPTER 5: TURKISH DELIGHT

1. How does temptation lead to sin? Explain the steps.
2. What basic elements of temptation are common among the stories of Digory and Edmund in Narnia, Eve in Eden, and Christ in the wilderness?
3. Edmund's desire for Turkish delight led him to sin. Since our desires lead us into temptation and sin, should we renounce all desires? Why or why not?
4. Are good and evil equal opposites? Why or why not?
5. Why is it impossible to commit evil strictly for its own sake?
6. Why is today's tendency to see ourselves as victims of our uncontrollable passions an affront to the way God created us?

CHAPTER 6: DEEP MAGIC BEFORE TIME

1. What parallels do you see between the death of Aslan and the crucifixion of Christ?
2. Did God have a plan already in place to rescue mankind if they sinned? Explain.
3. What parallels do you see between the broken Stone Table in Narnia and events surrounding Christ's crucifixion?
4. What parallels do you see between Narnia and the Gospels in the scene portraying Susan and Lucy's ministry to the Lion before and after his death?
5. Why did the boy Laurence (whose mother wrote to C. S. Lewis) fear that he loved Aslan more than Jesus? Why didn't Lewis think his concern was a problem? Do you agree with Lewis?
6. What does Aslan's love for his creatures show us about Jesus' love for us?
7. What Gospel accounts, other than the Crucifixion itself, show Jesus' love for people?

Chapter 7: Romping with the Lion

1. Narnia is filled with enormous joy. Why do you think many Christians seem reluctant to abandon themselves to great joy?

2. Do Christians derive any spiritual benefit from subjecting themselves deliberately to pain or discomfort? Why or why not?

3. Would you have been comfortable at the all-night party in *Prince Caspian* with its feasting, drinking, dancing, and yodeling with Bacchus and his wild girls? Why or why not?

4. Aslan approves of laughter at the "first joke" of the jackdaw. What do the many instances of humor in the Bible say about God's attitude toward fun and laughter?

5. Since God made all pleasures, can Christians rightfully enjoy all of them? Or are there exceptions? If so, what are they?

6. What is the difference between happiness and joy?

7. What did C. S. Lewis mean when he said, "Joy is the serious business of Heaven"?

Chapter 8: Slaying the Dragon Inside

1. What is the symbolic meaning of Eustace's becoming a dragon?

2. What is wrong with Bree's concern about his dignity when he rolls in the grass?

3. Do you see any connection between Bree's disbelief in Aslan as a real lion and his self-sufficient pride? Do you see any connection between this disbelief and the fact that he has lived so long outside the company of believers? Explain.

4. Why couldn't Eustace shed his dragon skin? Why can't we change our sin nature?

5. Why would Aslan not rid Eustace of his dragon nature until Eustace allowed him to do it?

6. What is the meaning of Aslan's throwing Eustace into the pool? What is the meaning of the new clothes he gives the boy?

7. Why didn't Eustace's behavior change totally for the better after Aslan undragoned him?

8. How did the apostle Paul express his battle with the dragon inside?

CHAPTER 9: FOLLOW THE SIGNS

1. Aslan gave a set of signs for Eustace and Polly to follow. What parallel do you see between those signs and our Christian life?

2. In what ways does God communicate his will to Christians today?

3. Why did Aslan use the two children and a marsh-wiggle to accomplish the rescue of the prince instead of doing it himself? Why does God use us in the same way?

4. Why weren't Aslan's signs always clear to the children and the marsh-wiggle? Why isn't God's will always clear to us?

5. Should we look for signs from God to find his direction in every situation? Why or why not?

6. Is rationalization ever a factor in our failure to understand God's will? Explain.

7. Releasing Prince Rilian could have put Puddleglum and the children in danger. If following God's will leads us into danger or difficulty, does he let us off the hook? Why or why not?

CHAPTER 10: ASKING ASLAN

1. After Caspian and his desperate followers blow the horn, it is days before the answer comes. What reasons can you give for the answer to prayers being delayed?

2. Is it selfish and unspiritual for a Christian to pray any kind of petitionary prayer? Why or why not?

3. What kinds of prayers are too selfish for God to answer?

4. When Aslan sends Digory on his quest, the boy wonders why food was not provided. Fledge suggests that the Lion wants to be asked. If God knows what we need before we ask, why does he want us to ask?

5. Digory thought briefly of bargaining with Aslan to get the silver apple he needed to heal his mother. Why isn't bargaining with God an effective way to get what we need or want?

6. If it's true that God can do anything, can he make two plus two equal five? Why or why not?

7. Why won't God answer prayers that violate the laws of nature or creation? Do healings violate these laws? Why or why not?

CHAPTER 11: ASLAN ON THE MOVE

1. When the prince tells Puddleglum and the children that one of the signs they followed was merely the chance workings of nature, Puddleglum responds, "There are no accidents." What did he mean? Do you agree?

2. It took centuries for the stone inscription to erode into Aslan's "Under Me" sign to direct Puddleglum and the children. What does this say about the intricacy of God working providence into nature?

3. What is the relationship of God to time and eternity? How does this relationship affect providence?

4. How can God accomplish his will on earth without violating our free will?

5. The book of Exodus says that God hardened Pharaoh's heart. Did God violate Pharaoh's free will in order to bring about his purpose? Explain.

6. Aslan frightens the horses Bree and Hwin into a burst of speed necessary to accomplish his purpose. He also scratches the back of Aravis. What do these acts show us about God's use of pain and fear to accomplish his purposes?

7. How can God's providence make us feel secure?

CHAPTER 12: FLYING YOUR FLAG

1. In what ways does Narnia resemble the Christian church?

2. Eustace and Edmund feel safe in confessing their most shameful sins to each other. What is the value of such confessions?

3. Eustace confesses to Jill, "Sorry I've been a funk and so ratty." Would his apology have been effective had he said, "Sorry *if* I've been a funk and so ratty"? Why or why not?

4. Is the purpose of the church to display the goodness of Christians? Explain your answer.

5. In Narnia each creature performs according to his or her own specialty. What is the value of our various abilities to the church? How does the apostle Paul express this?

6. When the various natures of the creatures threaten to throw Caspian's planning meeting into chaos, how is order restored? How does this apply to the church?

7. Why can't we be effective Christians apart from the church?

Chapter 13: The Blind Dwarfs

1. The dwarfs in *The Last Battle* refuse to believe in Aslan and heaven until they have empirical proof. Can everything commonly accepted as true be verified empirically? Explain your answer and give examples to support it.

2. Does our acceptance of the truth of Christianity require us to believe in spite of evidence? Explain.

3. The dwarfs have evidence of Aslan's existence and care, but they refuse to interpret it properly and remain firm in their disbelief. Is there empirical evidence to support atheism, or does it also require faith? Explain.

4. At first Edmund does not see the Lion that Lucy follows to lead the lost party to Prince Caspian. Yet he follows Lucy because he knows she is trustworthy. How does his decision exhibit the difference between merely having faith and exercising faith?

5. If rational argument seldom leads us to faith or shakes us from it, what can and more often does? Why?

6. What does the story of the Calormene Emeth in *The Last Battle* tell us about those who don't know Jesus? What does the apostle Paul say on this subject?

7. More than once in the Narnian stories Aslan says, "I tell no one any story but his own." What does this statement say about our judging who is saved and who is not?

CHAPTER 14: BEYOND THE SHADOWLANDS

1. In the Narnian stories a parallel realm exists above the natural lands in which the stories are set. Does this realm have any correspondence in our world? Explain.

2. How does Plato's illustration of shadows in a cave explain the natural and supernatural worlds? Does this illustration conform to the Christian understanding of earth and heaven?

3. In *The Last Battle* Aslan in the heavenly Narnia refers to the old Narnia as the Shadowlands. What does he mean?

4. Is the heavenly Narnia more or less substantial or "real" than the old Narnia? What does your answer say about the real heaven?

5. The witch in *The Silver Chair* explains to Puddleglum and the children that their belief in a better land above is naive make-believe, that it's all things from the lower world amplified and imagined bigger and better. What's wrong with this picture?

6. Nikabrik the dwarf in *Prince Caspian* rejects Aslan, yet he wants to call on supernatural powers. Why do many people who reject God still engage in spiritualism?

7. Do our acts here and now have any effect in the supernatural realm? In eternity? Explain your answer.

CHAPTER 15: FURTHER UP AND FURTHER IN

1. The Narnians are saddened as they witness the destruction of Narnia. How do you feel about the prophesied destruction of the earth?

2. What do you think heaven will be like? What is your source for these ideas? Do you look forward to living in this heaven?

3. The Narnians in the new Narnia have solid, flesh-and-blood bodies with their physical energy and stamina greatly enhanced. What kind of bodies do you think we will have in heaven?

4. Why did the old Narnia have to be destroyed? Why will our earth be destroyed?

5. Revelation speaks of a new heaven and a new earth. If we're expecting to go to heaven, what is the need of a new earth?

6. What is the meaning of Revelation 21:3, where we are told that God will make his tabernacle with men and dwell with them?

7. Will anything be forbidden in heaven? Explain.

CHAPTER 16: LONGING FOR ASLAN

1. Shasta yearns for the north, though he does not know why or what lies beyond the northern horizon. Have you ever experienced a desire for something you cannot explain or identify? Describe it as best you can.

2. Why does the object that stimulates a desire so often fail to satisfy it?

3. Narnians seem to have no trouble loving Aslan. Why do many of us find it so difficult to love God? How can we overcome this difficulty?

4. What evidences of God's love do you see in nature? In your life?

5. Aslan tells Lucy that the way into his country is across a great river, but not to fear because he is the great bridge builder. What is the meaning of the river and the bridge?

6. Aslan tells Lucy and Edmund that they must learn to see the things of Narnia in their own world. What did he mean?

7. Lucy realizes it's not Narnia she desires but Aslan himself. How can we come to realize that Jesus, rather than heaven, is the true object of our desire?

NOTES

PREFACE
1. C. S. Lewis, *Letters to Children*, ed. Lyle W. Dorsett and Marjorie Lamp Mead (1985; repr., New York: Macmillan, Collier Books, 1988), 35.
2. Ibid., 81.
3. Ibid., 45.

INTRODUCTION
1. C. S. Lewis, *Letters to Children*, 14.
2. C. S. Lewis, "On Three Ways of Writing for Children," in *On Stories and Other Essays on Literature*, ed. Walter Hooper (New York: Harcourt Brace Jovanovich, 1982), 35.
3. G. K. Chesterton, *Orthodoxy* (1908; repr. New York: Doubleday, Image Books, 1959), 50.
4. Lewis, "On Three Ways of Writing for Children," in *On Stories*, 35.
5. Ibid., 34.
6. Ibid., 31.
7. Humphrey Carpenter, *The Inklings* (1978; repr., London: Unwin Paperbacks, 1981), 65.
8. W. H. Lewis, ed., *Letters of C. S. Lewis* (New York: Harcourt, Brace & World, 1966), 287.
9. A. N. Wilson, *C. S. Lewis: A Biography* (New York: W. W. Norton, 1990), 196–97.
10. See J. R. R. Tolkien, "On Fairy Stories," in *Essays Presented to Charles Williams*, ed. C. S. Lewis (1947; repr., Grand Rapids: William B. Eerdmans, 1966); Lewis, "On Stories," "On Three Ways of Writing for Children," and "Sometimes Fairy Stories May Say Best What's to Be Said," in *On Stories*.
11. Lewis, "It All Began with a Picture . . . ," in *On Stories*, 53.
12. Lewis, "Sometimes Fairy Stories May Say Best What's to Be Said," in *On Stories*, 46.
13. Lewis, "On Three Ways of Writing for Children," in *On Stories*, 37.
14. Ibid., 38.
15. Lewis, "On Science Fiction," in *On Stories*, 63.
16. Lewis, "Sometimes Fairy Stories May Say Best What's to Be Said," in *On Stories*, 47.
17. Lewis, "On Stories," in *On Stories*, 10.

CHAPTER 1: NOT A TAME LION
1. C. S. Lewis, *The Lion, the Witch and the Wardrobe* (1950; repr., New York: HarperCollins, 1978), 74–75.
2. Ibid., 86.
3. Ibid., 140.
4. Dorothy Sayers, *The Mind of the Maker* (Cleveland: World Publishing, 1941), 91.
5. C. S. Lewis, *The Horse and His Boy* (1954; repr., New York: HarperCollins, 1982), 213–15.
6. C. S. Lewis, "Beyond Personality," in *Mere Christianity* (New York: Macmillan, 1952), 140.
7. Revelation 5:5.

8. Lewis, *Mere Christianity*, 120.

9. C. S. Lewis, *The Voyage of the Dawn Treader* (1952; repr., New York: HarperCollins, 1980), 174.

10. C. S. Lewis, *The Silver Chair* (1953; repr., New York: HarperCollins, 1981), 20–21.

11. Lewis, *Mere Christianity*, 39.

12. Lewis, *The Lion, the Witch and the Wardrobe*, 141.

13. Luke 14:26–27 NLT.

14. C. S. Lewis, *The Problem of Pain* (1940; repr., New York: Macmillan Paperbacks, 1962), 40.

15. C. S. Lewis, *The Magician's Nephew* (1955; repr., New York: HarperCollins, 1983), 168.

16. Lewis, *Prince Caspian* (1951; repr., New York: HarperCollins, 1979), 148.

17. John 11:35.

18. Matthew 23:37.

19. John 15:9, 15.

CHAPTER 2: THE SONG OF ASLAN

1. Lewis, *The Magician's Nephew*, 116.

2. Job 38:7.

3. Luke 19:40.

4. John 1:3. See also Colossians 1:16.

5. Lewis, *The Magician's Nephew*, 138.

6. Ibid., 140.

7. Genesis 1:28.

8. Lewis, *Prince Caspian*, 71.

9. Lewis, *The Magician's Nephew*, 117.

10. Genesis 1:31.

11. Lewis, *Mere Christianity*, 77.

12. Lewis, *The Magician's Nephew*, 177–78, 184–85.

13. Chesterton, *Orthodoxy*, 54.

14. C. S. Lewis, "The Weight of Glory," in *The Weight of Glory and Other Addresses* (1975; repr., New York: Macmillan Paperbacks, 1980), 18–19.

CHAPTER 3: MAMMALS, MOUNTAINS, AND MUFFINS

1. Lewis, *The Magician's Nephew*, 184.

2. Lewis, "On Stories," in *On Stories*, 13.

3. Lewis, *The Voyage of the Dawn Treader*, 258.

4. C. S. Lewis, *The Abolition of Man* (1947; repr., New York: Macmillan Paperback, 1955).

5. Lewis, *Prince Caspian*, 146.

6. C. S. Lewis, *The Last Battle* (1956; repr., New York: HarperCollins, 1983), 213.

7. C. S. Lewis, *Letters to Malcolm, Chiefly on Prayer* (New York: Harcourt, Brace & World, 1964), 17–18.

8. Ibid., 17.

9. 1 Corinthians 15:52–53.

10. Romans 8:21.

11. C. S. Lewis, *Reflections on the Psalms* (New York: Harcourt Brace & Company, 1958), 44.

CHAPTER 4: BAD MAGIC

1. Lewis, *The Magician's Nephew*, 56.
2. Ibid., 142.
3. Ibid., 161.
4. Lewis, *Mere Christianity*, 138.
5. Ibid., 37–38.
6. See Matthew 8:28–32.
7. Lewis, *The Silver Chair*, 177–78.

CHAPTER 5: TURKISH DELIGHT

1. Lewis, *The Lion, the Witch and the Wardrobe*, 39.
2. James 1:14–15 NLT.
3. Genesis 3:1, 4–6.
4. 1 John 2:16.
5. See Matthew 4:1–11.
6. Lewis, *Mere Christianity*, 106.
7. Ibid., 35.
8. C. S. Lewis, *The Screwtape Letters* (New York: Macmillan, 1942), 49.
9. Lewis, *Mere Christianity*, 35.
10. Lewis, *The Magician's Nephew*, 207–8.
11. Ibid., 169.

CHAPTER 6: DEEP MAGIC BEFORE TIME

1. Lewis, *The Lion, the Witch and the Wardrobe*, 155.
2. Romans 6:23.
3. Romans 3:23.
4. Lewis, *The Lion, the Witch and the Wardrobe*, 156.
5. Matthew 16:23.
6. Matthew 26:38.
7. Lewis, *The Lion, the Witch and the Wardrobe*, 170.
8. Ibid., 177–78.
9. Ibid., 178–79.
10. 1 Peter 1:20.
11. Lewis, *Mere Christianity*, 42.
12. Ibid., 141–42.
13. Ibid., 44.
14. Lewis, *Letters to Children*, 52.

CHAPTER 7: ROMPING WITH THE LION

1. Lewis, *The Lion, the Witch and the Wardrobe*, 179.
2. Luke 24:32.
3. See John 21:7.
4. Philippians 4:4.
5. Lewis, *The Magician's Nephew*, 161–62.
6. Ibid., 141.
7. Lewis, *The Lion, the Witch and the Wardrobe*, 199–200.
8. Lewis, *The Silver Chair*, 230–31.
9. Lewis, *The Horse and His Boy*, 238.
10. Lewis, *Prince Caspian*, 169.

11. C. S. Lewis, *That Hideous Strength* (1946; repr., New York: Scribner Classics, 1996), 313.

12. Psalm 150:3–5.

13. See 2 Samuel 6:12–23.

14. Mark 2:19.

15. 1 Samuel 21:15.

16. 1 Kings 18:27 NLT.

17. Roger Lancelyn Green and Walter Hooper, *C. S. Lewis: A Biography* (New York: Harcourt Brace Jovanovich, 1974), 229.

18. C. S. Lewis, *God in the Dock*, ed. Walter Hooper (Grand Rapids: William B. Eerdmans, 1970), 12.

19. Matthew 5:29.

20. Titus 1:15 NLT.

21. Galatians 6:2.

22. C. S. Lewis, "Membership," in *The Weight of Glory and Other Addresses*, 109.

23. W. H. Lewis, ed., *Letters of C. S. Lewis* (New York: Harcourt, Brace & World, 1966), 277.

24. Lewis, *Letters to Malcolm, Chiefly on Prayer*, 93.

25. Lewis, *The Silver Chair*, 154.

CHAPTER 8: SLAYING THE DRAGON INSIDE

1. Lewis, *The Voyage of the Dawn Treader*, 1.

2. Ibid., 97.

3. Lewis, *The Horse and His Boy*, 161–62.

4. Ibid., 216.

5. Isaiah 61:10.

6. Lewis, *The Voyage of the Dawn Treader*, 119–20.

7. Romans 7:18–23 NLT.

8. Romans 8:1–2 NLT.

9. Lewis, *Prince Caspian*, 220.

10. Luke 14:10–11.

11. See 2 Timothy 2:12; Revelation 5:10.

CHAPTER 9: FOLLOW THE SIGNS

1. Lewis, *The Silver Chair*, 10.

2. Douglas Gilbert and Clyde S. Kilby, *C. S. Lewis: Images of His World* (Grand Rapids, William B. Eerdmans, 1973), 67.

3. Lewis, *The Silver Chair*, 25.

4. Deuteronomy 6:6–7.

5. C. S. Lewis, "The Efficacy of Prayer," in *The World's Last Night* (New York: Harcourt, Brace & World, 1960), 9.

6. Lewis, *The Silver Chair*, 25–26.

7. Lewis, *The Lion, the Witch and the Wardrobe*, 65.

8. Lewis, "Answers to Questions on Christianity," in *God in the Dock*, 53.

9. Lewis, *The Silver Chair*, 154.

10. Lewis, *The Silver Chair*, 171.

11. Ibid., 24.

12. Ibid., 175.

13. Ibid., 250.

14. Matthew 25:21.
15. Lewis, *The Silver Chair*, 124.

CHAPTER 10: ASKING ASLAN
   1. Lewis, *Prince Caspian*, 99.
   2. Lewis, *The Voyage of the Dawn Treader*, 200.
   3. Matthew 21:22.
   4. See Matthew 10:29–31.
   5. Lewis, *Letters to Malcolm, Chiefly on Prayer*, 35.
   6. Matthew 6:9–13.
   7. Lewis, *The Magician's Nephew*, 178.
   8. Matthew 6:8.
   9. James 4:3.
   10. Lewis, *The Magician's Nephew*, 167–68.
   11. Ibid., 168–69.
   12. Lewis, *The Problem of Pain*, 28.
   13. Lewis, *The Voyage of the Dawn Treader*, 170.
   14. Matthew 26:39.
   15. Luke 22:43.
   16. 2 Corinthians 12:9.
   17. C. S. Lewis, *The Great Divorce* (New York: Macmillan, 1946), 69.

CHAPTER 11: ASLAN ON THE MOVE
   1. Lewis, *The Horse and His Boy*, 8.
   2. C. S. Lewis, *Miracles* (New York: Macmillan, 1947), 209.
   3. Lewis, *The Horse and His Boy*, 158.
   4. Lewis, *The Silver Chair*, 160.
   5. Lewis, *Mere Christianity*, 133.
   6. Lewis, *Miracles*, 208, 211–13.
   7. Of course, you know that these characters existed only in my head, and they could do only what I had them do. But as every fiction writer knows, once a character is created, she seems to gain independence in the mind of her creator. As the author deals with her and gets to know her, he often finds that she seems to have motivations and traits that cause her to make other choices and take other directions than those the author intended. It's an illusion, of course, but a common and persistent one among novelists.
   8. Lewis, *Miracles*, 211.
   9. Lewis, *The Silver Chair*, 141–43.
   10. Genesis 45:5.
   11. Exodus 7:13; 8:15; 8:32; 9:7; 9:34. These passages indicate that Pharaoh hardened his own heart.
   12. Sheldon Vanauken, *A Severe Mercy* (San Francisco: Harper & Row, 1977).
   13. C. S. Lewis, *The Problem of Pain*, 93.
   14. C. S. Lewis, "The Efficacy of Prayer," in *The World's Last Night*, 3.

CHAPTER 12: FLYING YOUR FLAG
   1. Lewis, *Prince Caspian*, 227.
   2. Galatians 6:2.
   3. Lewis, *The Voyage of the Dawn Treader*, 117.

4. Lewis, *The Silver Chair*, 201.
5. Lewis, *The Horse and His Boy*, 161–62.
6. Ibid., 228.
7. Galatians 3:28.
8. C. S. Lewis, "The Weight of Glory," in *The Weight of Glory and Other Addresses*, 19.
9. Lewis, *Prince Caspian*, 233.
10. Lewis, *The Magician's Nephew*, 133–35.
11. 1 Corinthians 12:17.
12. Lewis, *The Lion, the Witch and the Wardrobe*, 117–19.
13. Romans 12:6–8.
14. 1 John 1:7.
15. Lewis, "Answers to Questions on Christianity," in *God in the Dock*, 61–62.

CHAPTER 13: THE BLIND DWARFS
1. Lewis, *The Last Battle*, 184–85.
2. C. S. Lewis, "Religion: Reality or Substitute," in *Christian Reflections* (Grand Rapids: William B. Eerdmans, 1967), 43.
3. Ibid., 37–43; C. S. Lewis, "On Obstinacy in Belief," in *The World's Last Night*, 13–30.
4. Lewis, "On Obstinacy in Belief," in *The World's Last Night*, 13.
5. Lewis, *Mere Christianity*, 41.
6. Lewis, *Prince Caspian*, 156.
7. Lewis, "On Obstinacy in Belief," in *The World's Last Night*, 23.
8. Ibid., 26.
9. George MacDonald, "The Golden Key," in *The Gifts of the Child Christ*, ed. Glenn Edward Sadler (Grand Rapids: William B. Eerdmans, 1973), 171.
10. Lewis, *The Magician's Nephew*, 169–70.
11. Lewis, *The Last Battle*, 139.
12. Ibid., 205.
13. Matthew 25:31–44.
14. Romans 2:14–15 NLT.
15. Lewis, *The Last Battle*, 205–6.
16. Matthew 7:7.

CHAPTER 14: BEYOND THE SHADOWLANDS
1. Ephesians 6:12 NLT. See also Ephesians 3:10; Romans 8:38.
2. Lewis, *The Silver Chair*, 188.
3. C. S. Lewis, *The Four Loves* (New York: Harcourt, Brace & World, 1960), 142.
4. Lewis, *Prince Caspian*, 179.
5. Lewis, *The Last Battle*, 104.
6. Ephesians 6:12 NLT.

CHAPTER 15: FURTHER UP AND FURTHER IN
1. Lyle Smith, "Heaven," in *The C. S. Lewis Readers' Encyclopedia*, ed. Jeffrey D. Shultz and John G. West Jr. (Grand Rapids: Zondervan, 1998), 199. Lewis's imaginative images of heaven and unfallen paradises appear in *Out of the Silent Planet*, *Perelandra*, and *The Great Divorce*.
2. Lewis, *The Last Battle*, 197.

3. See 1 John 2:15–16.

4. Mark Twain, *Letters from the Earth* (1962; repr., Greenwich, Conn.: Fawcett Crest, 1966), 16.

5. Lewis, *The Last Battle*, 209–13.

6. Ibid., 228.

7. Ibid., 211–12.

8. Revelation 21:1; 2 Peter 3:12–13.

9. Revelation 21:2.

10. Revelation 21:3.

11. Revelation 21:5.

12. Lewis, *The Last Battle*, 224–25.

13. See 2 Timothy 2:12; Revelation 5:10; 22:5.

14. See 2 Peter 1:3–4.

15. Lewis, *The Last Battle*, 172.

16. 1 Corinthians 6:12.

17. Lewis, *That Hideous Strength*, 145.

18. Lewis, *The Last Battle*, 208.

19. Ibid., 213.

CHAPTER 16: LONGING FOR ASLAN

1. Lewis, *The Horse and His Boy*, 3.

2. C. S. Lewis, *Surprised by Joy* (New York: Harcourt, Brace & Company, 1955), 16.

3. Lewis, *The Last Battle*, 169.

4. Lewis, *The Voyage of the Dawn Treader*, 22.

5. Ibid., 231.

6. Ibid., 269–70.

7. Lewis, *The Last Battle*, 238.

KNOWING ASLAN

AN ENCOUNTER WITH THE LION OF NARNIA

THOMAS WILLIAMS

THE PERFECT
EVANGELISM TOOL
FOR CHRISTIANS
WHO WANT TO
SHARE CHRIST WITH
THEIR FRIENDS AND
NEIGHBORS.

I n addition to being one of the best-loved books of all time, *The Lion, the Witch and the Wardrobe* is sure to set box-office records when the movie releases Christmas 2005. Distributed by Disney, with special effects by WETA Workshop (*The Lord of the Rings*), and backed by a $150MM budget, *The Lion, the Witch and the Wardrobe* will draw millions of viewers, both Christian and non-Christian.

In the same way that Christians walked away from viewing Mel Gibson's *The Passion of the Christ* with a hunger to share Christ with their neighbors, Christians will leave *The Lion, the Witch and the Wardrobe* wanting to share the Christ depicted by Aslan in the movie. Aslan, killed by the White Witch and raised to life three days later, is a shadow of the One who was crucified and raised to life for our sins.

Using biblical parallels, this small, easy-to-read book will lead readers to an understanding of Christ and what He did for them by drawing lessons from The C.S. Lewis book and movie. Christians will want to buy this book in bulk as a non-threatening, warm-hearted evangelistic tool.

W PUBLISHING GROUP
A Division of Thomas Nelson Publishers
Since 1798
www.wpublishinggroup.com